THE Internal Family Systems WORKBOOK

An IFS Therapy Skills Training Manual for Beginners

—

Heal Trauma, Calm Anxiety & Inner Chaos, Build Confidence, and Nurture Self-Love and Your Inner Child

Disclaimer:

This content is for educational, entertainment, and informational purposes only. It is not intended to diagnose, treat, cure, or prevent any physical or mental health condition. Always consult with a licensed medical or mental health professional before trying any techniques described in this material. While every effort has been made to ensure the accuracy of the information, no guarantees are made. Individual results may vary. The author and publisher are not responsible for any losses or outcomes resulting from the use of this content, including errors, omissions, or inaccuracies.

Quotations & Sources:

Every effort has been made to credit the original sources of quotes and ideas used. Any unintentional omission will be corrected in future editions upon request.

Trademarks:

All trademarks, product names, company names, or logos mentioned are the property of their respective owners.

ISBN 9789083575421 (Paperback)

A Gift to Our Readers!

FREE DOWNLOAD ALERT!

Download and print our free **15-Day Mindfulness and Acceptance (Planner + Journal)!** Just go to https://life-zen.com/IFS to get your gift or scan the QR code on this page.

TABLE OF CONTENTS

A VISUAL INTRODUCTION TO INTERNAL FAMILY SYSTEMS (IFS)

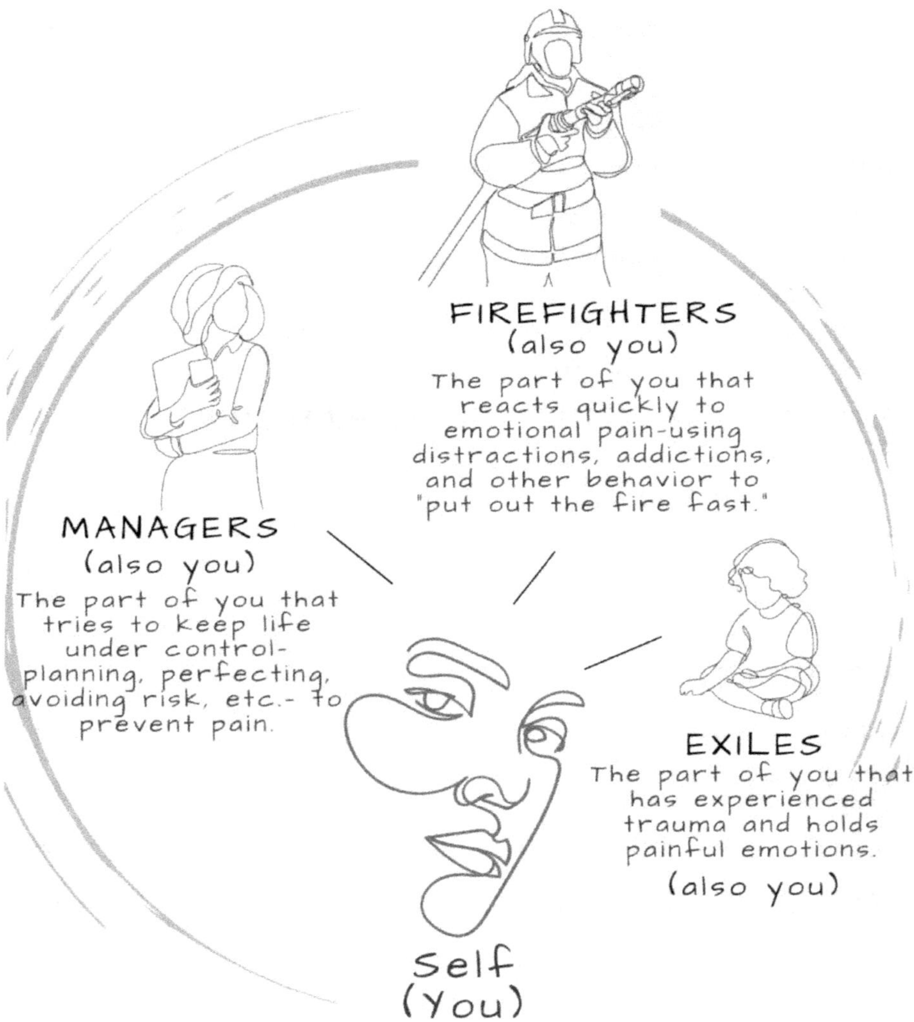

____

write your name here

Introduction

I'm all over the place!

I have one foot on the gas and one on the brake.

Why do I feel like I'm always arguing with myself?

Do any of these sound familiar? They most certainly do to me.

Many of my readers know that a couple of years ago, I went through burnout—the kind you can't just shake off with a yoga class or weekend getaway. And because I didn't take the time to understand what was actually happening inside me, that burnout spiraled into a full-blown nervous breakdown. Without a doubt, it was the darkest period of my life.

During that time, I always felt like I was arguing with myself.

I'm sooo tired.

Toughen up!

I'm ready for that presentation.

Am I?! I'd better check again.

I'm proud of what I did.

I could've done better.

I need a break.

Lazy, much?

All of this... it's just too much.

Hey, just walk away.

At my lowest of lows, while traveling for work and miles away from home, I suddenly found myself slumped on my hotel bed—crying like I had never cried before in my life.

I had this surreal out-of-body moment, almost like I was observing myself from a distance, thinking, *"Uh-oh... she's losing it, alright."*

Oddly enough, I didn't think I was going crazy. I've always thought that people have different sides to them—kind of like that classic Angel and Devil on your shoulder scenario.

But what was happening to me then was something else. It was louder, messier, and far more confusing.

At first, I thought I just needed more discipline, or maybe better boundaries. But the more I tried to trudge on, the more tangled I became inside. I was bone-deep tired, and absolutely nothing felt aligned.

I first consulted with a Dialectical Behavior Therapy (DBT) therapist because I was so impressed with its creator, Dr. Marsha Linehan.

Dr. Linehan had borderline personality disorder (BPD) and suffered severe mental health challenges in her youth. And yet, she was able to turn things around and go on to develop a new type of therapy to boot. So, I thought, "*If she could survive that, then there's hope for me too!*"

Looking back, I'm so glad I went with DBT because a crucial turning point in my journey was learning about DBT's *Radical Acceptance*. That concept changed everything for me.

I truly believe that unless we're willing to see and accept ourselves for who we are (warts and all), and acknowledge the reality of our circumstances (no matter how painful or unfair they may be) *without judgment or resistance*, real healing cannot begin.

You know, when you're deep into therapy, you can't help but learn about other approaches along the way. So, while I started with DBT, over time I began hearing about other therapeutic models—some in passing from my therapist, others through podcasts, books, and late-night internet rabbit holes.

I also started connecting with people in mental health forums and online support groups—many of whom were on their own healing journeys and swore by the effectiveness of *this* or *that* therapy or technique.

At first, all these "solutions" confused me. I kept wondering, *Why are there so many different therapies? Shouldn't there be just one that works?* But over time, I came to realize something important: there's no such thing as a "one-size-fits-all" solution when it comes to healing.

Humans are complex. We carry different wounds, different histories, and different ways of making sense of the world. What resonates deeply with one person might completely miss the mark for another. And so, it makes sense that we need different therapeutic frameworks—different languages of healing—to meet us where we are. Some of us need structure and skills. Others need space and softness. Many of us need a mix of both.

So I began to see therapy not as a single road, but as a landscape—with multiple paths that can intersect, diverge, and sometimes lead us to unexpected places. One of those unexpected places for me was **Internal Family Systems**, or IFS.

Honestly, at first, I just didn't get it. Different "parts" inside you? Is that like... multiple personalities? It sounded strange—maybe even a little woo-woo. But something about it tugged at me.

Maybe it was because I already felt like there were different "versions" of me inside—arguing and pulling in opposite directions. So much so that I was losing myself in the debate that was constantly going on inside me. And then it clicked...

IFS wasn't telling me I had different people inside me—it was showing me that I'm made up of different parts, and that each one is trying to help in its own way, even when it doesn't seem like it.

Think of it this way: **our physical body is made up of different parts**—head, arms, hands, legs, feet, etc. So **why wouldn't our inner world be made up of different emotional and psychological parts, too?** Each one with its own voice, its own story, and its own job to do.

With the above in mind, suddenly, the inner chaos I'd been experiencing didn't seem like chaos at all. It started to make sense.

- There was a part of me that pushed for perfection.
- A part that collapsed into exhaustion.
- A part that was tough and ready most mornings to take on the world.
- A part that cried in the bathroom at night and whispered, *"I can't do this anymore."*
- And in the middle of all these parts was something. A quiet presence. A center. A Self.

In many ways, IFS gave me a new way to meet myself—with curiosity instead of shame, and compassion instead of control. And that changed everything.

I realized that I didn't need to dismiss, ignore, or fight any inner voice or part inside me. What I needed to do was make these inner parts work together like a team!

And that's why I wrote this book. I want people to feel that same sense of *relief*—to finally stop feeling so exhausted by the noise inside them. People like me who:

- Feel like they have different voices inside (a frantic organizer, a harsh inner critic, a tired cheerleader, an overwhelmed and anxious adult, an angry teen, a scared child, etc.).
- Want to move on and get unstuck in life.
- Want to break free from negative thoughts and self-sabotaging patterns or habits.
- Want to heal from past hurts or trauma.
- Want to lead life from a place of calm, clarity, and confidence.

How to Use This WORKBOOK

Before you dive in, I want to offer you a gentle but important invitation: please try to **show up with curiosity, not certainty**.

Let go of the need to "get it right," and instead, focus on staying open—even when the material feels unfamiliar, uncomfortable, or challenging.

This isn't just a book to read. It's a space to engage with. Inside, you'll find reflective prompts, exercises, and guided worksheets throughout—because insight alone isn't enough. Real transformation happens when you apply what you've learned, one small, intentional step at a time.

Lastly, **let your participation with this book be a practice, not a performance**. Go at your own pace. And most of all be kind to yourself as you explore.

A Quick IFS Roadmap

IFS is amazing—life-changing, even—but if this is your first time learning about IFS, it can feel a bit like stepping into a big, bustling city without a map. There are new terms, new ways of thinking, new ways of looking at yourself, and a whole new way of unpacking your inner world.

To help you, here's a simple IFS roadmap to help you think of this journey like learning to navigate a new city inside yourself. (Note that this is just an overview, not the full process.)

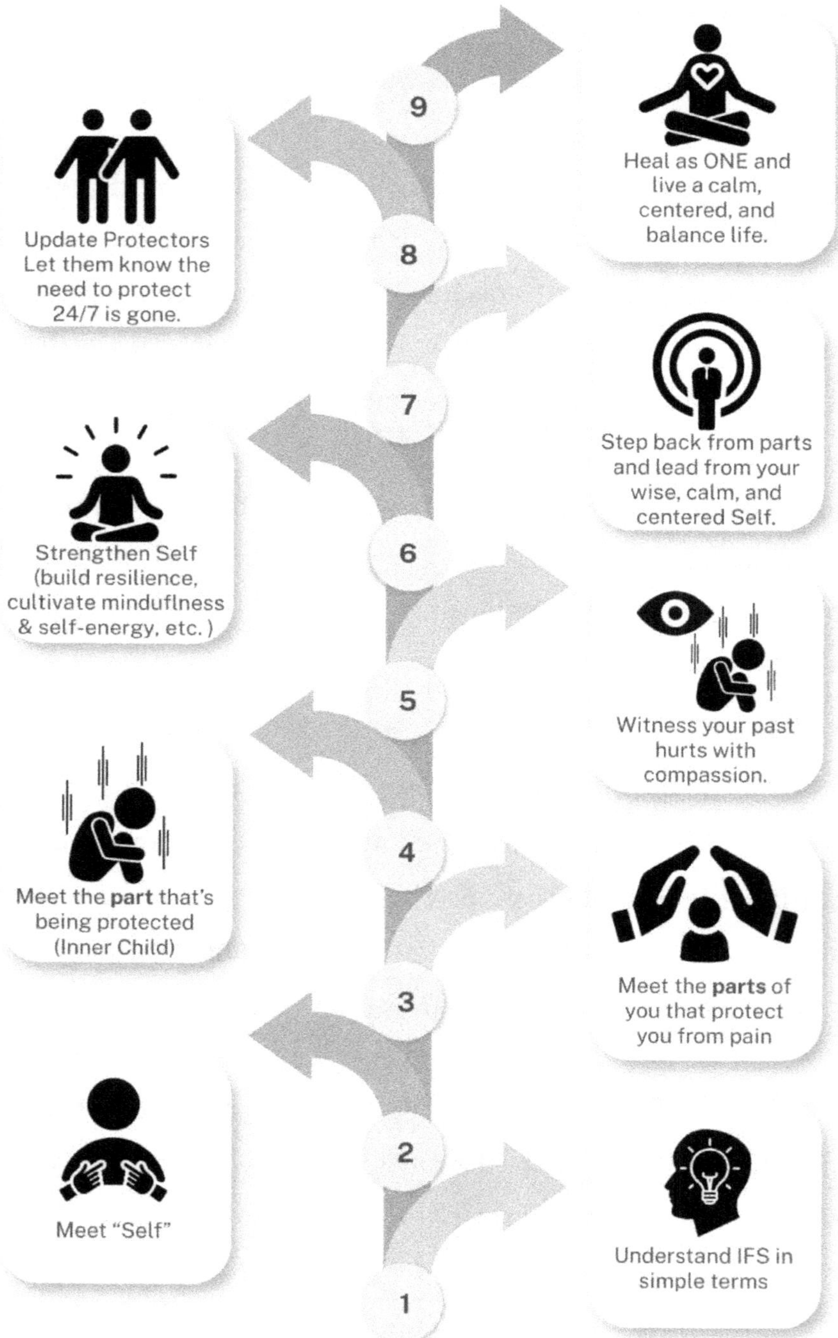
9
Heal as ONE and live a calm, centered, and balance life.
8
Update Protectors Let them know the need to protect 24/7 is gone.
7
Step back from parts and lead from your wise, calm, and centered Self.
6
Strengthen Self (build resilience, cultivate minduflness & self-energy, etc.)
5
Witness your past hurts with compassion.
4
Meet the **part** that's being protected (Inner Child)
3
Meet the **parts** of you that protect you from pain
2
Meet "Self"
1
Understand IFS in simple terms

Give Yourself Patience and Kindness

IFS may hit deep, and at times, it can stir up more than you expected. You might feel stuck one day and open the next. You might uncover parts of yourself that surprise you—or even challenge how you see yourself entirely. And that's okay!

Growth in this kind of inner work is never linear. Some parts of you may jump on board right away, while others resist or withdraw. All of that is part of the journey.

So please, be gentle with yourself. Meet every part of you with curiosity, not judgment. And when things feel messy or hard, offer yourself the same kindness you would give a struggling friend.

So, dear reader, are you ready to meet yourself and all the parts that make you unique?

Let's start.

Ava Watters

Amazon Bestselling Author

Survivor

What is IFS?

"Happiness is not a matter of intensity but of balance, order, rhythm and harmony."— Thomas Merton

Internal Family Systems or IFS therapy was developed by Dr. Richard Schwartz in the 1980s. Dr. Schwartz was working as a family therapist at the time and noticed something... interesting.

His clients often spoke about *parts* of themselves as if they were different people or family members living inside them. Some parts felt anxious, some felt angry, and some just wanted to protect themselves from pain. Curious about this, he started listening more closely to these "inner family members."

Dr. Schwartz discovered that these different *parts* weren't just random feelings—they had their own needs, fears, and roles. He also noticed that, much like in any family, these parts sometimes argued or didn't get along. Other times, they worked together to help the person feel balanced and safe.

Over time, Dr. Schwartz realized that we all have an "inner family" and our internal family members develop as we grow, shaped by our experiences and our environment.

Some parts of us are like protectors—tough and serious, always on guard. Others are more vulnerable, carrying our pain and hurt. And deep inside all of us is something special called "Self."

Needless to say, Dr. Schwartz's approach was very different from traditional models of therapy at the time. While others focused on "fixing" seemingly unhelpful parts, IFS therapy sees these parts as important *messengers*—each with something valuable to share.

So, IFS therapy isn't about ignoring or fixing certain parts of you—it's about learning to gently honor ALL your parts, no matter how loud or quiet, helpful or unhelpful they might seem. Why? Because **every part of you has a reason for being there**—even the ones that seem destructive or confusing.

Now, you might be thinking, *"If the point of IFS is to acknowledge ALL my parts? Why should I know more about each one of them?* Because acknowledgment of the whole is just the first step—creating a *relationship between them* is what brings healing.

Here's the thing: your internal family members (or parts) developed to protect you, to help you cope, or to carry pain that you subconsciously cannot handle.

So, getting to know your parts helps you understand why they act the way they do, what they're afraid of, and how they've been trying to help you (even if their methods are outdated or extreme).

When you build a relationship with your parts, you move from reacting automatically to responding consciously. You begin to lead your inner system with more clarity, compassion, and confidence—and that's when real transformation happens.

So learning more about your parts isn't just informative—it's empowering. It gives you the inner map you need to navigate life with more self-trust and emotional freedom.

A Tale of Two Friends, Two Different Inner Family Systems

Imagine two friends, Sam and Jordan, who both feel nervous about speaking in front of a group.

Sam's inner family system includes a very confident part that says, "*You've got this! Just be yourself.*" He also has a quiet, shy part that sometimes worries about looking silly. A part that says,

"Oh boy, I might mess this up." But Sam's parts usually work well together, so even if he's nervous, he can still feel calm and steady, and do what he needs to do.

Jordan's inner family, on the other hand, is a little different. He has a very strong inner critic that says, *"Don't mess up! You have to be perfect. Otherwise, you'll look like an IDIOT out there and you'll never live that down."*

He also has an anxious part that feels like everyone's watching and judging him all the time. Now, when these parts get LOUD, Jordan feels stuck and overwhelmed. As a result, Jordan might never step out of his comfort zone.

IFS can help Jordan by giving him a way to listen to his parts with kindness and curiosity. Instead of trying to shut his parts down or push them away, he might learn to say, *"I see you, Inner Critic. I see you, Mr. Anxiety. And I know you're just trying to protect me."*

From there, Jordan can begin to build trust with those parts—understanding that the critic isn't trying to be mean, it's trying to keep him safe from shame. And the anxious part isn't trying to make him weak; it's just vigilant because it's scared of being hurt.

Why This Matters

As you can see from these two tales, IFS therapy isn't about fixing you or trying to shut your inner voices. It's about seeing that even your loudest, messiest feelings are there—for a reason.

Your inner parts are just trying to help you in the best way they know how. And with a little patience and curiosity, you can learn to bring them together like a family—so they can support you, instead of pulling you apart.

The Core Concepts of IFS

In this chapter, we'll discuss the core principles of IFS to give you a sense of how they fit together.

The Self: Your True, Wise Center

At the heart of IFS is the awareness of the **Self**—a calm, wise, and compassionate center that's always there, even if it feels hidden at times.

The Self is the part of you that can listen to your thoughts and feelings. It's the part of you that can pay attention to what's going on inside you.

Here's a common everyday example of "Self" in action:
You're feeling overwhelmed after a tough day and part of you wants to snap at someone, while another part just wants to hide under the covers.

But instead of reacting either away, you take a deep breath, pause, and say to yourself, *"It's okay, calm down. The day's almost over."*

THAT moment of calm awareness—the ability to notice your feelings without being swept away by them—is your Self in action.

It's the You, the Leader, who can hold space for all your parts with compassion, curiosity, and clarity.

Internal Family Members (a.k.a., Internal Family Parts or Parts)

IFS therapy supposes that we all have different *parts* inside us—each with its own feelings and goals. These parts aren't there to hurt us. In fact, they're all trying to help in the best ways they know how.

First, you have the **Protectors**:

- **Managers** are *proactive* Protectors. They work hard to plan, organize, and control things to keep you safe and avoid pain. They might push you to be perfect, to take care of everyone else, or to stay one step ahead of problems.

  For example, suppose you have a big presentation coming up. In this case, a

Manager part might kick in, keeping you up late rehearsing every detail, rewriting your slides ten times, and obsessing over what others might think—because it believes that being 100% prepared will protect you from embarrassment or criticism.

Takeaway: Managers show up to prevent pain *before* it happens—by keeping things under control, avoiding risk, and ensuring everything (including you) looks "okay" on the outside.

It's the part of you that thinks:

If I stay busy, no one will notice I'm struggling.
If I get everything right, I won't get hurt.
If I take care of everyone else, maybe I'll be safe too.

A Manager part doesn't wait for a crisis—it works hard behind the scenes to prevent one from ever happening.

- **Firefighters** are *reactive* Protectors. They jump in fast when intense feelings or old wounds bubble up, distracting you or numbing you out so you don't have to feel that pain. They might push you to overeat, shut down, get angry, or check out completely.

For example, say you get a critical email from your boss, and it stirs up deep feelings of "not being good enough." Almost instantly, a Firefighter part takes over, and before you know it, you're reaching for a bag of chips, slumping on the couch, and binge-watching on Netflix.

Takeaway: Firefighters show up *after* pain has occurred, and their sole purpose is to put out emotional fires—fast.

It jumps in when pain, fear, or old wounds and trauma start to surface and says, *"Nope, we're not going there!"* Its goal is to stop you from feeling overwhelmed, even if that means distracting, numbing, or shutting things down completely.

It's the part of you that thinks:

Quick—grab your phone, eat something, do anything—just don't feel this.
Let's blow up, shut down, or check out—whatever it takes to make the pain stop.
This is too much. We're out.

So, we have **Protectors** inside us. But, who or what are they trying to protect? The **Exiles**.

Exiles are the parts of you that carry your deepest hurts and fears. Exiles hold the pain of past experiences that feel too big to handle. They're often the tender, childlike parts of you that still feel shame, fear, emptiness, or loneliness.

Your Protectors (Managers and Firefighters) work hard to keep Exiles out of your awareness—because they believe that if you had to feel those old wounds, it would be too overwhelming, too painful, or too harmful for your well-being.

However, our Exiles never really go away, do they? Exiles are always there, waiting for a chance to be seen and healed.

What's the Real Value of IFS? What Do You Gain?

Your inner world is not just a collection of parts—it's a **system**. And like a family, these parts have their own relationships and ways of working together. Sometimes they get along smoothly, and other times they clash or feel stuck.

For example, suppose you send a text to someone you really care about, but they don't respond for hours. Immediately, your **Manager part** jumps in: *"Don't act needy. Just play it cool. You probably said too much—next time, keep it short."* It's trying to protect you from feeling rejected.

But as the hours drag on, a wave of insecurity and sadness starts to rise inside you—that's your **Exile**, the part of you that remembers what it feels like to be ignored, left out, or not chosen.

But before your Exile's feelings get too strong, your **Firefighter part** steps in and says, *"Hmpf! Whatever. Who cares? Let's go order a bucket of chicken and demolish it."* You might then impulsively block the person, ghost them back, or pour yourself one too many glasses of wine—*anything* to avoid feeling that sting of hurt.

Now, **in a balanced system, the Self leads** with calm and compassion, helping each inner family member (inner part) feel heard and cared for. Here's an example:

Trigger: Suppose someone makes a comment about your weight in public.

Manager part (proactive protector): *Okay, hold it together. Smile. Smile! Don't let them see it got to you.*
Self: *It's okay—we don't need to pretend. Let's just take a deep breath here, and...*
Exile part: *I feel so ashamed! I've felt this way since middle school. I want to disappear.*
Self: *Hey, I hear you. That hurt runs deep. But you're not alone anymore.*
Firefighter: *Screw them! Let's go home, eat everything in the fridge, and block them on every app.*
Self: *I get it. You're trying to protect us from pain. But we don't need to numb out—we need care. Why don't we choose something that truly supports us right now?*

In this example, the Self leads and calms every inner part down. Outwardly, this results in less emotional overwhelm, fewer impulsive reactions, and a deeper sense of inner safety.

However, when Self is not quite strong enough to lead yet or is unequipped to lead, it can feel drowned out. This is because the Managers and Firefighters get so busy trying to protect the Exile that there's no room left for Self to show up.

(In IFS terms, we say that the Self is ***unavailable*** *in these moments, usually because other parts are so activated that they take over the system.).*

In these moments, it can feel like you're just emotionally reacting to the noise inside, and not acting or behaving from a place of calm, clarity, compassion, and logic.

Here's another example: Imagine you're in an argument with your partner about how little time they've been spending with you lately.

Your partner says:
"I've been working late. I'm not ignoring you. I just don't have any time to spare."

The minute you hear this, a part of you that feels hurt or rejected starts to bubble up—this is an **Exile**, carrying old wounds of feeling unseen or unimportant.

Sensing that pain rising, your **Firefighter** jumps in to shut it down—*fast*—by getting angry.

Before you know it, words fly out of your mouth that you don't really mean—harsh, sharp words meant to protect you from feeling that deeper hurt.

You (Firefighter-led) snap back:
"Oh, please. You always have some excuse. Just admit you don't care anymore!"
Partner (feeling hurt):
"That's not fair."
You (Firefighter-led):
"Not fair?! You know, what's not fair? Me holding everything together—taking care of the house, the kids, our schedules—while you come and go like it's no big deal! You know what? Never mind. I'm used to handling EVERYTHING anyway."

In the heat of the moment, there's no calm or logic—just a reaction. And as soon as it's over, you feel that wave of regret wash over you. You might think, *"Why did I say that?!"*

In the above example, a **Protector** (in this case, a Firefighter) completely took over—leaving no room for your wise, calm Self to come out and lead.

So, to visualize, ***before IFS***, your internal world may look like this, a common reality where the **Protectors have taken over** and Self is exiled along with the Exiles.

Think of all the times you did or said something you immediately regretted, or reacted in a way that didn't feel like "you." If this happens every now and then, that's okay but if you find yourself often in this situation, chances are **Protectors have taken the lead** and your **Self isn't in charge**.

Real-world consequence: When Protector parts are in charge, you're often reacting from a place of emotion rather than clarity.

As such, your decisions may feel impulsive, overly defensive, avoidant, or disconnected from your deeper values. **You might say things you don't mean, agree to things you don't want, or avoid situations that actually matter to you**—because the goal of the Protectors is to *manage pain*, not necessarily to make thoughtful choices.

Over time, this can lead to strained relationships, burnout, guilt, or feeling like you've lost touch with who you really are.

Here's another example of what your inner world might feel like before IFS work.

In the above scenario **your system is flooded with pain or is in crisis.**

Think of times when you felt completely overwhelmed—like a wave of panic, shame, grief, or heartbreak crashed over you—and you couldn't think straight, breathe deeply, or calm yourself down. In response to these overwhelming emotions, maybe you lashed out, shut down, numbed out, or isolated.

That's often when an **Exile part has taken over**, flooding your system with old pain that was never fully processed—and your other parts (particularly, Firefighter parts) are scrambling to protect you however they can.

Real-world consequence: When Exile parts are in charge, you may feel **emotionally hijacked**—like you're drowning in sadness, fear, or shame with no way out. It's not just discomfort; it's **emotional flooding**. This can make even small tasks feel impossible, strain your relationships, and leave you exhausted or confused about why you're reacting so intensely.

Over time, when intense emotions are left unmanaged and your system stays stuck in survival mode, it can lead to **emotional shutdown, chronic stress, burnout, or depressive symptoms**.

In some cases, people experience what feels like a **nervous breakdown**—not because they're broken, but because their system has been overloaded for too long without support.

So, **what's the real value of IFS?** What will you gain from this inner work? **A balanced inner system, led by Self.**

When you live a life that's **Self-led**, you make decisions with clarity, respond to challenges with calm, and relate to yourself and others with compassion.

And that's the real gift of IFS—a life that feels more balanced, grounded, intentional, and truly your own.

IFS Controversies Galore!

Internal Family Systems has gained a lot of praise—but it's not without its critics. In this chapter, we'll take an honest look at the common concerns, misunderstandings, and debates surrounding IFS therapy. Why? Because it's better to understand them, rather than to write off a powerful therapy because of a few misconceptions.

Controversy #1: IFS Feels a Little "Woo-Woo|

Some people feel that IFS, with its idea of "inner parts" talking to you, sounds a bit too abstract or mystical. It might feel silly or hard to believe at first, especially if you're used to more traditional, logic-based approaches.

But then again, who hasn't heard of the classic "Angel and Devil on your shoulder" analogy, right? So, if you think about it, we've *always* had ways of describing our internal conflicts.

IFS simply takes that common experience and gives it structure, language, and a path forward. It's not about fantasy—it's about mapping the real, complex emotional landscape inside us all.

How to better see this: Try thinking of "parts" as ways of describing your feelings and thoughts. Instead of taking it literally, see them as metaphors that can help you better understand why you feel what you feel. This can make it easier to work with your emotions, even if the idea of "inner family parts" feels odd at first.

Controversy #2: IFS Can Seem Like You're Making Excuses for Bad Behavior

Some critics worry that listening to parts might make it easy to say, *"It's not me, it's just my part,"* and avoid responsibility.

The truth: IFS doesn't let you off the hook—it's about understanding and owning what's going on inside you. If a part is pushing you to do things you don't like or, at your core, don't even agree with, your job is to listen and understand—not to blame the part. Remember, Self is the leader, and you get to decide how you act in the world.

Controversy #3: Hocus Pocus! There's No Hard Science Behind IFS

IFS has a lot of support from people who've used it, but there isn't as much research compared to older therapies like Cognitive Behavioral Therapy (CBT) or Dialectical Behavior Therapy (DBT). Some therapists or researchers feel that IFS just doesn't have enough scientific proof yet.

The truth: Yes, IFS is still growing in research, but that doesn't mean it doesn't help. Even CBT was met with skepticism when it first emerged in the 1960s and 70s.[1]

At the time, many clinicians were rooted in psychoanalysis or behavioral conditioning, and the idea that simply changing your thoughts could change your emotions and behavior seemed overly simplistic or unproven. However, over time, research caught up, methods evolved, and CBT became one of the most well-studied and widely used therapies in the world.

IFS is on a similar path—starting with theory and clinical intuition, and now steadily building its evidence base through studies on trauma, PTSD, anxiety, depression, and even chronic illness.[2,3,4] Like any emerging model, it takes time for the science to catch up with the practice.

Bottom line, if it feels helpful and healing to you, that's what matters most! I truly believe that when it comes to mental health, any therapy you can genuinely relate to can work for you.

Controversy #4: IFS Can Feel Overwhelming or Confusing

For some people, especially if they have a lot of parts or past trauma, diving into IFS work can feel overwhelming or chaotic at first.

How to make this work for you: Go slowly. You don't have to meet every internal family member all at once. Start with gentle curiosity. Maybe spend a few minutes each day just noticing how you feel and writing down any voices or feelings you notice. This can help you build a relationship with your parts at a pace that feels safe. (More on this in Chapter 2: Meeting Your Inner Family.)

To be honest, when I first started learning about IFS, I wasn't intimidated by the idea of having "parts." I actually felt sort of *excited* to discover them.

For as long as I could remember, I'd felt pulled in different directions, stuck in patterns I couldn't explain. I was a people-pleaser and suffered from imposter syndrome.

So, a part of me worked overtime to keep everyone happy—even if it meant ignoring my own needs. Another part constantly worried I'd be "found out," like I didn't really belong in the rooms I was in. And then there was a quieter part that just wanted to disappear when things got too overwhelming. This inner tug-of-war left me exhausted!

So when I learned about IFS, it made something inside me exhale. I thought, *"Finally! Here's a way to put into words what I'd been feeling all along. I'm not broken, unhinged, or unbalanced. It's just that different parts of me were trying to protect me in different ways."*

Controversy #5: It's Hard to Do IFS Alone

Some people find it tricky to practice IFS on their own. It can feel easier with a therapist who can guide you through the process. And since therapy can be expensive, many stay clear of IFS.

The truth: You can absolutely explore IFS concepts on your own. Even just getting to know your parts can be extremely liberating! And if at any point you feel stuck or uncertain, working with an IFS-trained therapist can be a helpful next step.

Working with a Therapist vs. Self-Therapy

In IFS, healing happens when you connect with your parts from your calm, wise Self. But how you do this—whether with a therapist or on your own—can look a little different.

When you work with a therapist, their main role is to guide you and create a safe, supportive space. They help you slow down and really listen to your parts without getting overwhelmed.

A therapist can notice patterns you might miss and help you find words for things that feel confusing or scary. They're also there to make sure you feel grounded and safe, especially if you're working with parts that carry deep pain.

Self-therapy, on the other hand, is something you can do at home—like journaling, meditating, doing the worksheets in this book, practicing gentle curiosity about your feelings, etc. You're still the one leading the way, but you might do it without another person in the room. Many people find self-therapy powerful and freeing. Why?

You see, some people who go to therapy secretly fear judgment—even from the most well-meaning therapist. They worry about saying the "wrong" thing, being misunderstood, or feeling exposed. As such, they might "filter" or "shape" what they share, rather than be 100% authentic. (This is known in therapy as "impression management.")[5,6]

In those cases, self-therapy can be a softer entry point: it allows you to explore at your own pace, in your own words, without filtering or performing for someone else. It's not a replacement for therapy, but it can absolutely be a meaningful part of your healing process.

Here's what's important to remember: whether you're doing this work on your own or with a therapist, the goal is the same—helping your Self develop into the leader that's capable of acknowledging, hearing, and caring for your Protectors and Exiles.

Controversy #6: I Have "Bad" Parts?!

One of the biggest misunderstandings people have about IFS is the idea that our parts are somehow bad or broken. It's easy to see them this way, especially if you have a part that's critical, anxious, or reactive. You might think, *"This part is causing me problems! I need to silence it."*

But **here's what IFS gently teaches us: You have no bad parts.[1] You have protective ones.**

When you look closely at what your parts are doing, you'll see they're actually trying to help. They're like your own personal team, each with a job. Some parts work hard to keep you from feeling pain. Others carry old hurts that they're still trying to manage. Even the loud, angry parts usually show up to keep you safe—because deep down, they believe you need protecting.

It doesn't mean their ways of helping always work well. Sometimes they push you too hard *(Manager: Oh, come on! What's two more kilometers?)* or they keep you stuck in habits that don't serve you anymore *(Firefighter: You know you always feel better after you've had a slice of chocolate cake.)*. But their intentions are always to protect you, not to harm you.

[1] *"No Bad Parts" is another amazing book about IFS by Richard C. Schwartz.*

So, when you stop seeing your parts as "bad" and start seeing them as protectors, you open the door to healing. Instead of fighting or ignoring them, you can start listening to them. You can thank them for trying so hard to help, and work with them to find new, healthier ways to care for you.

This shift—seeing your parts as protective rather than bad—can bring you more kindness, patience, and understanding. It's one of the first steps to building a more balanced and peaceful relationship with yourself.

Controversy #7: False Memories

One controversy people sometimes mention about IFS is the idea of "false memories." Here's what that means...

When you do deep inner work, like talking to your parts and exploring old hurts, you might remember things you haven't thought about in a long time. Some of these memories can feel very vivid and emotional.

The controversy comes from the idea that, during therapy, some memories that come up might not be entirely accurate. They might be "false memories" or memories that feel real but didn't actually happen, or happened differently. This can be especially tricky when people have a history of trauma, because the brain can fill in gaps to make sense of what happened.

How to better see this: If you're working with memories in IFS (or any therapy), remember that your feelings and reactions are always real and deserve care, no matter what.

You don't have to "prove" or "disprove" a memory to find healing. Focus on how your parts feel now and what they need today, rather than getting stuck in whether every detail of a memory is 100% true.

IFS encourages you to trust your inner experience while staying curious and gentle. You don't have to turn memory work into detective work—healing is about helping your parts feel heard, supported, and safe.

A Note about Mental Health Disorders

IFS therapy is a wonderful and gentle way to explore your inner world, but it's important to remember that if you have a mental health disorder such as PTSD, bipolar disorder, severe depression, or any other serious condition, doing deep IFS work on your own can sometimes feel overwhelming or even unsafe.

These conditions can make it harder to separate your parts from your core Self. You might feel like certain parts are so loud or powerful that you can't get enough distance from them to work with them calmly.

If this sounds like you, don't worry. It just means you might need extra support and guidance. IFS can still help, but it's usually best to work with a trained therapist who understands your unique situation and can help you go at a pace that feels safe.

Remember: You deserve help and support. Your feelings and struggles are valid, and you're not alone. If you ever feel stuck or scared while exploring your parts, reach out to a mental health professional. Healing doesn't have to be a solo journey, and it's always okay to ask for help.

IFS vs. Other Therapies

When you first hear about IFS, it might sound very different from other types of therapy. So let's take a closer look at how it compares to some common and popular approaches.

Unlike **Cognitive Behavioral Therapy (CBT)**, which focuses on changing unhelpful thoughts and behaviors, IFS doesn't try to "fix" your thinking directly. Instead, it helps you see that those thoughts come from parts of you that are trying to protect you. Rather than arguing with these thoughts, IFS encourages you to understand and listen to the parts that hold them.

Mindfulness practices such as those used in Acceptance and Commitment Therapy (ACT) and Mindfulness-Based Stress

Reduction (MBSR) encourage you to notice and accept your thoughts and feelings in the present moment.

IFS builds on mindfulness practices by showing you that these feelings and thoughts often *belong* to parts of you that need care and compassion. While ACT and MBSR help you "make space" for difficult feelings, IFS helps you actively befriend and heal the parts behind those feelings.

Dialectical Behavior Therapy (DBT) is another popular approach. It teaches practical skills (i.e., mindfulness, distress tolerance, emotion regulation, and interpersonal effectiveness) to help people handle difficult emotions. DBT also focuses on balancing acceptance with change. In other words, it helps you say, *"This is where I am right now,"* while also asking, "*What small steps can I take to get to where I want to be?"*

While IFS doesn't have a set of skills training exercises like DBT, it can still help you handle intense emotions by giving each part a safe place to share and be heard.

Somatic therapy focuses on how your body holds and expresses your memories, experiences, and emotions. It helps you tune into physical sensations as a path to healing.

For example, suppose you've been suffering from constant migraines for years. Somatic therapy wouldn't just look at that single physical symptom—it might also explore other ways you manifest tension, stress, or unprocessed emotions. In doing so, you might begin to notice that your shoulders always tense up during conflict, or that your jaw clenches when you feel unheard.

By bringing awareness to those patterns—and learning how to release them gently using body-based movement—somatic work can help your body, nervous system, and mind find relief.

In IFS, you also pay attention to your body's signals—but the goal is to understand the *part* behind the sensation. For example, if you've been feeling tightness in your chest, the next step is to gently ask: *Which part might this belong to?*

Does it belong to a part of you that feels anxious and afraid of being judged (Exile)? Or does it belong to a part that's trying to keep you from speaking up to avoid conflict (Firefighter)?

In short, the sensation is the doorway—but the deeper work is in connecting with the part that's carrying the tension, listening to its concerns, and responding with curiosity and compassion.

Another big difference is how IFS talks about your **Self**.

In IFS, the Self is your natural center of calm, wisdom, and compassion. **Self is always there—it's not something you have to create or imagine.** IFS helps you connect with your Self so you can lead your inner system, instead of letting anyone part take over.

Traditional talk therapy might explore your feelings or memories through conversation, but IFS offers a gentle way to interact directly with your parts. It helps you understand why each part does what it does, and how to help it feel safe enough to let go of old roles that no longer serve you.

And at the heart of IFS is this simple idea: **every part of you has a reason for being there.**

Even the parts that cause you the most pain are trying to help in some way. When you see them not as problems to be fixed, but as protectors and messengers, healing becomes more about understanding and kindness.

Therapy Approach	Key Focus	How It Works	Best For
IFS (Internal Family Systems)	Understanding and healing your inner parts	You explore your parts, listen with curiosity, and connect with your calm, wise Self.	Feeling stuck in old patterns; tired and drowning from the chaos inside; wanting to heal parts of

Therapy Approach	Key Focus	How It Works	Best For
			yourself instead of "fixing" them.
CBT (Cognitive Behavioral Therapy)	Changing negative thoughts and behaviors	You challenge unhelpful thoughts and practice new, healthier behaviors.	Struggling with habits, negative thinking, or needing practical tools to reframe thoughts.
ACT (Acceptance and Commitment Therapy)	Accepting difficult feelings and living by your values	You practice mindfulness, accept thoughts and feelings, and take action that matches your values.	Feeling stuck in thoughts, wanting to align life with personal values, and needing clarity on life direction.
DBT (Dialectical Behavior Therapy)	Managing intense emotions and relationships	You learn specific skills: mindfulness, emotion regulation, distress tolerance, and better communication skills.	Handling big emotions, self-harm, or relationship struggles; wanting more structure and clear tools.
Somatic Therapy	Releasing emotional pain stored in the body	You pay attention to body sensations and let the body guide the healing.	Feeling physically tense or holding stress in your body; wanting body-focused healing.

Preparing for IFS Work

"Before every deep transformation, there is a pause—a moment to gather strength, breathe, and come home to yourself."— Anonymous

It's easy to *meet* someone. You say, "*Hi*," they say, "*Hello.*" You say your name, they mention theirs, and you may even share a smile. But to really get to *know* someone—earning their trust, hearing their stories, understanding their fears and hopes—that takes time, patience, and effort.

The same is true with IFS work.

You see, you're not just doing surface-level self-reflection here. You're going to get to know the deeper, more complex *parts* of yourself—the ones that have been carrying pain, working behind the scenes, or staying hidden to protect you.

Why does that take effort?

Because we **humans are masters at tucking things away**! We carry old shame like a secret we forgot we were keeping. We silence parts of ourselves that were once judged, rejected, or overwhelmed. And over time, those parts retreat—not because they're bad, but because they didn't feel safe to be seen. They make us feel vulnerable, so we do our best to bury them deep within our psyche.

So, before you begin working with your parts, it's important to slow down and create the conditions that make inner connection possible. Because just like anything in life, **preparation makes the IFS journey smoother, safer, and more meaningful**.

Now, you might be thinking, *"I'm the one asking myself questions, so why all the prep and care?"*

You might have never considered it, but here's the truth: **it can be quite uncomfortable to reveal yourself—even to yourself**.

When you "tuck away things" and avoid certain thoughts, downplay certain feelings, or bury old memories, these are protective strategies that become habits over time.

So when you start turning inward, even gently, it can stir discomfort. You might feel resistance, judgment, or even fear—not because you're doing something wrong, but because you're not used to looking at *parts* that have been kept quiet for so long.

Note: *If this feels overwhelming, consider beginning this process with the support of someone you trust. If that person is a friend or family member rather than a professional, let them know ahead of time that strong emotions might come up. That way, they won't be caught off guard, and you'll both be prepared to pause.*

Think of this chapter as setting the foundation for slow and meaningful inner work.

Just like you'd prepare a room before inviting guests over, you're preparing your *inner space* to welcome the parts of you that may have been ignored, pushed aside, or overwhelmed.

You'll be guided through simple but powerful practices like setting clear intentions, creating a sense of safety, tracking your inner experience, and cultivating present-moment awareness.

Mind you, these aren't just "warm-ups." They're essential tools for approaching IFS work with care and clarity.

Bottom line, you cannot bulldoze your way into healing.
It begins with **welcoming**.

Setting Your Intentions

Let's start by thinking about what you really want from IFS. Setting your intentions doesn't have to be complicated—it's simply about clarifying why you're here and what you hope to find.

Maybe your intention is to feel less stuck or overwhelmed. Maybe you want to understand why you react the way you do. Or maybe you're just curious to see what's happening inside you. Whatever your intention is, it's valid. There's no right or wrong reason to begin with IFS.

Here's a simple reflection exercise for you:

Take a moment to sit somewhere quiet. Let your body relax, and take a few slow, calming breaths. When you're ready, ask yourself:

What drew me to IFS?

Example: I'm tired of the constant tug-of-war of opinions inside me.

____

____

____

What am I hoping to understand or heal?

Example: I'm hoping to find more calm and balance within myself.

____

____

____

How do I want to treat myself and my parts as I begin?

Example: I want to treat myself and my parts with patience and kindness.

____

____

____

As you reflect, you might notice words or images that come to mind. You can write them down, speak them out loud, or just hold them gently in your mind.

If you'd like, finish this sentence in a way that feels true for you:

My intention for this work is to...

Example: Better understand my inner world. I want to meet my parts and comprehend WHY they react the way they do. I also want to explore how I can strengthen my Self so it can step up as a true inner leader—because honestly, I often feel lost and scattered inside.

____

____

____

____

____

____

____

____

____

____

Remember, **your intention doesn't have to be perfect or final**. It can change as you learn more about your parts and yourself. What matters most is that it comes from your heart—something that feels true and gentle, and that helps you feel safe to begin.

Creating a Safe Space

When you're working with your parts in IFS, creating a safe space for yourself is one of the most important things you can do. This isn't just about finding a quiet room—it's also about helping your parts feel protected and welcome.

You might start by choosing a comfortable spot where you won't be disturbed. Maybe you have a favorite chair or a cozy blanket you like to wrap around you.

Some people find it helpful to play soft music or light a candle while doing inner work. The idea is to create an environment that feels calm and soothing for you and your parts.

Creating a safe space is also about your **inner environment**.

So, before you begin, you might want to tell your parts: *"I'm here to listen, not to judge. This is a time for understanding, not for fixing or forcing anything to change."* This can help your parts feel more willing to show up and share what they're holding.

Remember, your parts might need a little time to trust that this space is truly safe. That's okay. Go slowly. Let them know they don't have to share more than they're ready for. You can even ask them, *"What would help you feel safe right now?"* and then just patiently wait and see what comes up.

Tracking Your Journey

As you begin your IFS work, it can be helpful to track your journey. This doesn't mean you need to measure or "score" yourself—it's more about noticing how things shift and change over time.

You might find that some parts of you open up quickly, while others take a little longer to feel safe and heard. You might have days when you feel really connected to your calm, wise Self, and days when it feels harder to find that place of peace. All of this is normal. Remember, healing isn't a straight line—it has ups, downs, and many detours along the way.

One way to track your journey is to keep a simple journal, take notes on your phone, or use a notetaking app like Evernote, Simplenote, GoodNotes, or Apple Notes.

After each IFS chapter you've read or worksheet you've done, you can reflect and write down:

Which parts showed up today?
What did I learn about these parts?
How did my Self feel during this time?
What small shift or insight did I notice?

Over time, you'll see that even small changes add up. You might notice that a part that used to feel stuck or scared now feels a little more open or curious. Or you might see that you're better able to pause and listen to your parts, even when things feel hard.

Tracking your journey helps remind you that this work matters. It shows you that, step by step, you're building more understanding and compassion for all the parts of you. And that's something worth celebrating.

Mindfulness: Coming Home to the Present

Mindfulness is one of THE most important skills I learned in my healing journey.

Like most folks, **I thought mindfulness was a waste of time**—until I realized that all my efforts to heal kept falling flat because I wasn't actually present in the moment. My mind was either lost in the past or bracing for the future. And without awareness in the moment, nothing could really land or shift.

Think of it this way: **before you can fully accept what's happening inside you, it helps to start by simply noticing it**. Not noticing in passing; not noticing in a distracted way; not noticing in a hurry; but noticing with all your senses. And when you notice, you do so without trying to change them or push them away. That is mindfulness.

In IFS work, mindfulness is like a gentle anchor. **It helps you stay in touch with your calm, wise Self.** It allows you to notice your parts when they show up, without getting swept up in their stories.

I also like to think of mindfulness like a "mental pause." When things around me or inside me feel big or messy, mindfulness helps me remember...

I can handle this.

I can stay present.

I can just be.

Worksheet 1: Mindful Breathing and Grounding

This mindful exercise is made up of three progressive parts to help you gently connect to your body, breath, and the present moment. It's especially useful before beginning any internal work with parts, emotions, or difficult memories.

However, at this stage, don't think of IFS or any inner work just yet. Just focus on being still or letting yourself be. Once you're used to quieting your mind, you'll find that IFS work becomes smoother and easier.

Estimated time: 10–15 minutes
This exercise can be done seated or lying down, eyes open or closed.

Short on time? No problem. You don't have to complete all three parts at once. Even choosing *just one*—a few breaths, a short grounding, or a quick sensory check-in—can help you settle and feel more present.

Part 1: Mindful Breathing

Time: 3–5 minutes

Start by simply **noticing your breath**. You don't need to change it—just observe it.

- *Inhale* and notice the air entering your nose.
- *Exhale* and feel the air leaving your body.

Let your attention gently follow your breath in and out.

If your mind wanders—that's okay. Gently bring it back to your breath without judgment. Think of this as an internal "home base" that you can return to at any time.

Try this for a few cycles of breath, allowing yourself to arrive more fully in the moment.

Part 2: Counting the Breath

Time: 3–5 minutes

Next, we'll bring a gentle structure to the breath to help anchor your attention.

Practice:

- Inhale slowly and count "**one**" in your mind.
- Exhale slowly.
- Inhale again, and count "**two**" in your mind.
- Exhale slowly.
- Inhale again, **"three."**

Continue this pattern until you reach **ten**. Don't be surprised, but in all likelihood, somewhere along the way, you'll get lost, distracted, and forget your counting before you reach "ten." If you have time, start over with "one." If you don't, that's okay.

The goal is to eventually breathe to **ten** mindfully, being fully aware of each breath.

Part 3: Grounding Through the Five Senses

Time: 5 minutes or longer

Now that you're more connected to your breath, let's bring your awareness to the world around you using your **five senses**. Take your time with each one. You can say these aloud or silently.

👀 **Sight:** Look around and name **5 things you can see**.

Example: I see the light on the wall, the wallpaper behind it, the pattern in the rug, the shape of the chair, and my coffee mug.

✋ **Touch:** Notice **4 things you can feel**.

Example: The texture of my shirt, the air on my skin, the chair supporting my back, and my slightly itchy socks.

👂 **Sound:** Listen and **name 3 things you can hear**.

Example: A car passing, a bird, the hum of my computer.

👃 **Smell:** Breathe in and **notice 2 smells**, strong or faint.

Example: The scent of soap and the smell of paper.

👅 **Taste:** Bring awareness to **1 thing you can taste**.

Example: The taste of toothpaste in my mouth.

Reflect (Optional Journal Prompts):

- What was the hardest part to do or stay focused on?
- What part of this exercise helped you feel the most grounded or present?
- Was there a part of you that resisted slowing down?
- How might this kind of check-in help before doing deeper emotional work?

Radical Acceptance: Embracing Where You Are

Radical Acceptance is a powerful concept from Dialectical Behavior Therapy (DBT) that invites you to fully acknowledge your present reality—*without judgment, blame, or resistance.*

That might sound simple, but it's often one of the hardest things to do! Why? Because we're used to resisting what we don't like—trying to fix it, figure it out, avoid it, or mentally rewrite it. Our minds are constantly scanning for what's wrong, what should be different, or how we can escape discomfort.

Ever heard the phrase "*get out of your own way*"?
That's what Radical Acceptance helps you do.
Because when you're constantly fighting what *is,* it's easy to stay stuck. You loop in frustration:

"This shouldn't be happening."
"I can't believe I let that happen."
"Things would be fine if only..."

See, what I mean?

So, I like to think of Radical Acceptance as simply **Reality Acceptance**.

It's not about giving up. It's about pausing the internal war long enough to say: *"This is what's true right now. I may not like it. I may want it to change. But this is where I am."*

And ironically, **true change starts from that moment of acceptance**—not from denial, shame, or blame, but from awareness.

What has Radical Acceptance got to do with IFS work?
A lot, actually.

In IFS, you're learning to build relationships with your inner parts—some of which may carry pain, fear, anger, or shame. If you approach those parts with judgment, resistance, or an agenda to "fix" them, they'll likely stay guarded or hidden.

Radical Acceptance invites you to meet each part exactly as it is—without blame, without resistance, and without trying to make it go away.

When you accept what's real in the moment—whether it's a racing heart, a judgmental inner voice, or a memory that won't let go—your energy shifts. You're no longer stuck in a tug-of-war between how things *are* and how you *wish* they were. That frees up space for healing, clarity, and Self-leadership.

In other words, Radical Acceptance is what helps your parts feel safe enough to step forward. And it's what helps your Self step into the lead—with compassion, curiosity, and calm.

Try This: Think about something in your life you wish were different. It could be big or small—something recent or long-standing.

Now, repeat the following sentence (even if you don't fully believe it yet):

"This is what's true right now. I don't have to like it—but I'm willing to accept it."

Notice what comes up. A part of you may want to reject that sentence completely. Another part might feel relieved.

That's okay. Acceptance isn't a one-time decision—it's a practice. One breath, one moment, one piece of reality at a time.

Worksheet 2: I Accept

Use this worksheet anytime you want to ground yourself in Radical Acceptance before diving deeper into your parts work.

Step 1: Find a quiet space. Sit somewhere comfortable. Take a few slow, steady breaths and feel the weight of your body in the chair or on the floor.

Step 2: Notice what's here. Ask yourself gently:

What feelings are here with me right now?
How does my body feel in this moment?
Am I feeling any resistance whatsoever? Physically, mentally, or emotionally?

Step 3: Name what you see. Without judging or trying to change anything, simply name what's there. You might say:

I feel tightness in my chest.
There's a part of me that feels scared.
I'm noticing a voice that says, "I don't want to do this."

Step 4: Offer kind words. Speak to yourself with gentle understanding:

"This is what's here right now, and that's okay."
"I don't have to fix this. I can just notice and be with it."

Step 5: Let Go of the need to control. See if you can let go of the urge to force yourself to feel differently. Remind yourself:

"I don't have to like how I feel right now, but I can accept that it's what's true in this moment."
"It's safe to be with what's here."

Step 6: End with a small act of kindness. Before you finish, ask yourself: *"What's one small thing I can do to care for myself right now?"*

Maybe it's taking a deep breath, stretching your body, or simply saying, *"I'm doing the best I can."*

Somatic Awareness: Listening to Your Body

Your body often speaks before your mind can put words to it. As such, one very powerful way to learn and connect with your inner family member (*parts*) is by tuning into your body—this is called somatic awareness.

You see, your parts don't just live in your mind; they often show up as physical sensations, such as tightness in your chest, a sinking feeling in your stomach, hairs standing on your arms or at the back of your neck, tension in your shoulders, and others.

When you pause and bring gentle attention to these sensations, you can start to get curious about which *part* of you might be showing up.

For example, you might notice that a fluttering feeling in your stomach comes from a nervous part that wants to keep you safe. Or heaviness in your chest might be a sad part that's been carrying an old hurt for a long time.

Think of it this way: instead of trying to meet a *part* and asking, *"Who are you and what do you want?"* you start by paying attention to your body's signals or messages and say, *"I'm here. I'm listening. What do you need me to notice?"*

Somatic awareness in IFS means tuning into **body sensations** as invitations. By listening to your body, you create a softer, more intuitive path to meeting the part *behind* the sensation.

Worksheet 3: Somatic Awareness

Somatic awareness is the practice of noticing what your body feels—without rushing to interpret, fix, or change anything. Your body is constantly giving you information, but many of us have learned to ignore or override those signals. This exercise helps you begin tuning back in.

Step 1: Settle in (1–2 minutes). Find a comfortable position—sitting or lying down. Allow your hands to rest gently on your lap or by your sides. Take 2–3 slow, gentle breaths.

Let your shoulders drop, unclench your jaw, and soften your gaze or close your eyes.

Step 2: Scan your body slowly (4–5 minutes). Begin at the top of your head and slowly bring your attention downward.

Move through each area of your body:
Head → Face → Neck → Shoulders → Chest → Arms → Belly → Back → Hips → Legs → Feet

As you move through each area, pause and ask gently:
What do I notice here?
Is there tension, tightness, lightness, warmth, coolness, tingling, numbness, or nothing at all?

Remember: There's no need to change anything—just notice. If you feel nothing in a certain area, that's okay. Noticing *nothing* is also awareness. If your mind wanders, simply return to the next area of your body.

Step 3: Choose one sensation to stay with (3–5 minutes). Once you've scanned your whole body, gently bring your attention to one area or sensation that stood out to you.

It could be something subtle or strong (e.g., tightness in your shoulders, warmth in your chest, heaviness in your legs, etc.).

Sit with that sensation for a few minutes and explore it gently with curiosity. Ask yourself:

Where exactly is this sensation located?
Does it stay the same, or does it shift over time?
Is it moving, pulsing, sharp, dull, still, heavy?
Can I breathe into this area without trying to change it—just being with it?

Think of yourself as an observer—noticing without analyzing or judging.

Step 4: Gently come back (1–2 minutes). When you feel ready, slowly bring your awareness back to the room.

Wiggle your fingers and toes, and gently stretch if needed. Open your eyes if they were closed. Take one final deep breath. You might say silently: "*I am here. I am present in my body.*"

Somatic awareness isn't about making sense of your sensations or turning them into a story. It's about reconnecting with the physical experience of being *in* your body.

Like any skill, the more you practice it, the more natural it becomes. So, try to spend even just a few minutes a day on his exercise to build a deeper sense of grounding, calm, and inner connection.

Meeting Your Inner Family

"Getting to know the voices inside you isn't crazy. It's clarity." —Brené Brown

In this chapter, we will dig deep into your **internal family system**. Now, this might sound a little unusual at first—after all, you probably think of *family* as the people you grew up with, not the feelings and thoughts inside you. But in IFS, this idea of an "inner family" is central to understanding yourself—and learning how to respond rather than just react.

Confused? Don't be. Let's start with the classic "Angel and Devil on your shoulder" analogy.

Situation: You're dreading an important responsibility like calling someone back.
Angel: *"Call. Do the right thing and do it now. You'll feel better afterward."*
Devil: *"Who cares? They don't deserve your effort. Just blow it off."*

And then, there's the "inner dialogue," those silent *conversations* you have with yourself when trying to make a decision or anticipate how a situation might play out. It's a natural, everyday process.

Here's an example:

Situation: You need to call someone and let them know you won't be able to make it to their party.
Voice 1: *"Call. Do the right thing and do it now. You'll feel better afterward."*
You: *"But what do I say....?"*
Voice 2: *"Just blurt it out. Say you can't make it."*
You: *"Sounds harsh. I should at least give some reason."*
Voice 2: *"Say anything you want. It doesn't really matter, does it?"*
Voice 3: *"Just be ready. You don't want to be persuaded into coming."*
You: *"Yeah, I don't want that."*
Voice 3: *"Remember... boundaries."*
Voice 1: *"But call NOW so you don't have to dread it all week."*

So, as you can see, the idea of having *different* inner voices is not new. What IFS does is take this one step further by:

- Identifying these inner voices as **"parts"** of you—each with its own role and perspective,
- Encouraging you to **listen and understand** those parts rather than ignore, silence, or judge them.

- Helping you reconnect with your **Self**—the calm, clear, compassionate center of you—so that you can respond with wisdom instead of reacting from (internal) chaos.

Why is it so important to reconnect and strengthen your Self? Because someone needs to lead.

Think of it this way: your inner family is just like any other family. And have you ever met a family that gets along perfectly all the time? Exactly.

Without leadership, things get loud, chaotic, or tense inside. Your parts need someone steady—someone who can listen, mediate, and guide. That someone is you—your **Self.**

Many years ago, I was attending a leadership conference, and the Speaker asked, *"What type of leader is the best type of leader?"* Many replied, and the Speaker diplomatically replied with something like, *"That's good. That's one way to look at it."*

The Speaker then swung with his microphone, looked directly at me, and asked the same question. From out of nowhere, I said, *"The best type of leader depends on the type of members they have."*

So, dear reader, let's go and meet the internal family members you have.

Managers: Your Inner Organizers

Imagine you're getting ready for an important meeting at work. There's a voice in your head that says, *"Double-check your notes. Make sure you look professional. Don't let anyone see you're nervous."* This voice might keep you up late the night before, rehearsing over and over, just to make sure everything's perfect.

Or picture a busy, harassed housewife juggling a hundred tasks in a single morning—getting the kids ready for school, wiping down the counters, making sure the laundry is on, and keeping track of everyone's schedule. There's a voice in her head that says, *"Don't let anything fall through the cracks! You have to keep this together!"*

These are the Manager parts at work.

Managers are like the inner organizers or supervisors in your system. They want to make sure you're prepared, safe, and in control of what's happening around you. They're always planning ahead, fixing problems before they happen, and pushing you to be your best.

Manager parts can show up in lots of ways. This means that you can have multiple manager parts, with each one having a different approach to managing emotional distress.

Common Types of Manager Parts in IFS

Everyone's Manager parts will look a little different, so just see which one(s) resonate with you.

- **The Perfectionist** – Always pushing you to do everything perfectly and to avoid mistakes.
- **The Inner Critic** – Keeps you in line by pointing out flaws and what's "wrong."
- **The Planner** – Loves to make lists, organize everything, and prepare for every possibility.
- **The Achiever** – Sets high goals and pushes you to always do more and be better than yesterday.
- **The Caretaker** – Focuses on making sure everyone else is okay, even at the expense of their own needs.
- **The Controller** – Wants to manage everything and everyone to prevent surprises or mistakes.
- **The People-Pleaser** – Works hard to keep others happy and will do almost anything to avoid conflict or rejection.
- **The Rule-Follower** – Keeps you safe by sticking to rules, traditions, or what's expected.
- **The Doubter** – Questions every decision to keep you from making a "bad" choice.
- **The Researcher** – Gathers lots of information to make sure you're always prepared and informed.

- **The Hard Worker** – Always busy, never resting, afraid of slowing down.
- **The Avoider** – Tries to prevent risky situations by staying small or invisible.
- **The Stoic** – Keeps feelings hidden to stay strong and "in control."

Manager parts can be loud and busy, or quiet and watchful. And as you can see, each has its own reason for showing up and trying to protect you.

Important: In IFS, Manager parts aren't there to make your life harder. They're not "pushing" for the sake of pushing or running you down. They're trying to keep things running smoothly to *prevent* problems. Why? Because if problems occur, you might get hurt or feel deep pain.

Here's a metaphor that might help: Think of Managers as strict parents who want to keep you safe! And just like any strict parent, they may come across as a big pain in the *ss at times, but in the end, you know they do it out of love.

So, instead of fighting or clashing with your Managers, why not start to listen to them with curiosity and compassion instead? Discovering why they work so hard to protect you might help them feel safe enough to lie low.

Worksheet 4: Getting to Know Your Inner Managers

This simple exercise will help you start to notice and understand the Manager parts that show up in your life.

Important: You don't need to figure out all your Manager parts with this exercise—that comes later. This is just something to help jumpstart your curiosity about your Manager parts. If at any point this feels overwhelming, pause. You can come back to this at a later time.

Step 1: Find a quiet space. Sit somewhere comfortable and take a few slow, steady breaths. Let your body settle. Remind yourself that there's no rush—this is just about gentle noticing.

Step 2: Recall a recent stressful situation. Think of a moment when you felt under pressure—maybe at work, with your family, or even with yourself. Close your eyes and let that situation come to mind.

Step 3: Notice the voices or urges inside you. Ask yourself:

What were the voices in my head saying?
Was there a voice telling me to be perfect, to plan ahead, or to make sure everyone else was okay?

Did I feel a sense of needing to control or keep everything together?

Step 4: Name the Manager part that showed up. If you notice a voice or feeling, see if you can give it a simple name or description. For example:

- ☐ **The Perfectionist**
- ☐ **The Inner Critic**
- ☐ **The Planner**
- ☐ **The Achiever**
- ☐ **The Caretaker**
- ☐ **The Controller**
- ☐ **The People-Pleaser**
- ☐ **The Rule-Follower**
- ☐ **The Doubter**
- ☐ **The Researcher**
- ☐ **The Hard Worker**
- ☐ **The Avoider**
- ☐ **The Stoic**
- ☐ **Other:** ______________________________

If you're not sure what to call it, just describe how it feels. For example:

"The part that's always pushing me to do more."

"The part that shuts down when things feel too overwhelming."
"The part that's always worrying about what others might think."

Step 5: Get curious about its role. Gently ask this part:

What are you trying to help me with?
What are you afraid would happen if you didn't work so hard?
How long have you been doing this job for me?

Don't worry if you don't hear clear answers right away—just notice what feelings or images come up.

Step 6: Thank your Manager part. Before you finish, thank this part for what it's trying to do for you. You might say to yourself:

"Thank you for looking out for me."
"I see how hard you're working to keep me safe."
"Thank you for caring about me, even if it's hard sometimes."

Step 7: Record your insights. Jot down in your journal or on your note-taking app:

The name or feeling of the Manager part

Example: I think the Manager part that showed up was the Inner Critic. It gave me a feeling of tightness in my chest and pressure to be perfect—like I had to get everything right or else I'd disappoint someone.

____

____

____

____

Anything you noticed about what it wants or fears?

Example: It seems like my Inner Critic wants me to avoid failure or rejection. I think it's afraid that if I make a mistake, people won't respect me. Or worse, they'll abandon me.

____

____

____

____

How is it trying to help you?

Example: It tries to help by pointing out everything I did wrong before anyone else can. In its own way, it believes this pressure will protect me from shame.

____

____

____

____

Firefighters: Your Inner First Responders

Imagine you've just had a stressful day at work. You're feeling hurt and rejected because your boss criticized your idea—in front of everyone.

As you're driving home, a voice inside you says, *"Let's just stop at that fast food place and eat something comforting."* Or maybe another voice says, *"I need a drink to take the edge off tonight."* Sometimes, you might notice yourself zoning out on the couch, binge-watching a show until you can't feel anything anymore.

These are your **Firefighter** parts at work. They're the first responders in your inner world—rushing in to stop the pain as soon as it flares up.

The Firefighter's job is to distract, numb, or shut down the pain, even if it's just for a little while. And like Manager parts, they come in many forms.

Some push you to eat, drink, or shop. Others might get loud and angry, picking fights to cover up the hurt. Some just want you to disappear—turning off your feelings completely so you don't have to face them.

But no matter how they show up, Firefighter parts always have the same goal: **to keep you from feeling the raw, deep pain buried underneath.**

Unfortunately, the Firefighter usually doesn't take time to evaluate what's going on—**it just reacts**. So, whatever the Firefighter encourages you to do, it's often a short-term solution. That is, you're encouraged to do something NOW to get *temporary relief* from emotional distress.

Here are some examples of **Firefighter behaviors**:

- **Escapism.** When things feel too overwhelming, your Firefighter parts might push you to find any distraction that takes you away from the pain. This could mean:

    - Scrolling on social media for hours.
    - Playing video games or watching TV until you feel numb.
    - Overbooking your schedule so you're never alone with your thoughts.

- **Soothing.** Sometimes your Firefighters want to soothe you when the pain feels too raw. They might want you to:

    - Reach for comfort foods and eat more than you need, just to feel a little relief.

- Pour a drink (or several) to take the edge off.
- Use substances or anything else that helps you not feel so much.

- **Impulsive Actions.** Firefighters can also push you to act out fast and intensely, so you don't have to sit with difficult feelings. This might look like:

  - Spending money impulsively.
  - Getting into heated arguments or yelling at someone close to you.
  - Making decisions that feel reckless in the moment—like driving too fast or taking unnecessary risks.

- **Shutting Down.** Other Firefighter parts might just want to shut everything off completely. They might:

  - Make you feel numb or disconnected from your emotions.
  - Lead you to sleep for long stretches to escape what's happening.
  - Leave you feeling like you're "checking out" or "floating away" from yourself.

- **Overworking.** Some Firefighters use work or busy-ness as a way to cope. They might:

- Push you to stay busy all day so there's no time to feel.
- Keep you jumping from task to task to avoid quiet or stillness.
- Make you feel like resting is dangerous or unsafe.

As you can see, these behaviors might not seem helpful in the long run, but your Firefighters are always trying to protect you from something that feels too painful to face. They're saying, *"Let's not go there right now. Let's do something else so you don't have to feel that pain."*

When you start to understand this, it opens the door to healing. You don't have to fight or silence your Firefighter parts. You can begin to listen to them with curiosity and compassion, seeing the pain they're trying to help you avoid.

And as you build trust with them, you'll find that they can soften, making more space for your calm, wise Self to lead.

Worksheet 5: Exploring Your Firefighter Behaviors

This worksheet will help you notice your Firefighter patterns and understand how they try to help.

Important: You don't need to figure out all your Firefighter behaviors with this exercise—that comes later. This is just something to help jumpstart your curiosity about your Firefighter parts. If at any point this feels overwhelming, pause. You can come back to this at a later time.

Step 1: Find a quiet, comfortable space. Settle into a chair or find a cozy spot where you won't be interrupted. Take a few slow breaths and let your body relax. Remind yourself: this is a safe, gentle exploration.

Step 2: Recall a recent moment of overwhelm. Think back to a time when you felt stressed, hurt, or overwhelmed.

Where were you?

Example: I was in the kitchen trying to get dinner ready while my phone kept buzzing with work emails. My kids were arguing in the next room, and I felt like everything was closing in on me.

____

____

____

____

____

How did your body feel in that moment?

Example: My chest got tight, my jaw clenched, and I felt heat rising in my face. My breathing became shallow, and I noticed my shoulders were tense and scrunched up toward my ears.

____

____

____

____

____

Step 3: Recall what you did next. Ask yourself:

What did you do right after that moment?

Example: I saw the pot of pasta water starting to boil over, so I grabbed the lid and threw it hard on the sink. It made a loud sound.

____

____

____

____

____

Did you reach for food, your phone, turn on the TV?

Example: I threw exactly three pieces of chicken nuggets in the air fryer to snack on.

____

____

____

____

____

Did you lash out at someone, or shut down completely?

Example: Both, I think. My 8-year-old came into the kitchen, startled by the lid I not-so-gently put down, and asked me if anything was wrong. I said "Nothing" a bit too loudly, and that was that.

____

____

____

____

____

Step 4: Explore the feeling behind the behavior. Gently ask yourself:

What do you think you were trying to avoid feeling?

Example: I don't know. I guess I was trying to avoid the feeling that I was falling apart, like I couldn't handle anything else.

____

____

____

____

Was there a part of you that felt too much pain, fear, or shame in that moment?

Example: More like just "too much" of everything. As if too many things were coming right at me. Looking back now, I think I felt like a "target" or something.

____

____

____

____

What feeling or state do you think your Firefighter hoped to achieve by prompting you to react the way you did?

Example: Relief? I think slamming the pot lid was like shouting "Stop!" like "Stop coming at me," or that I just want not to be needed by anyone for a minute.

____

____

____

____

Step 5: Name the Firefighter behavior that came out in your recollection.

Look back at what you wrote. See if you can give a simple name or description to the Firefighter behavior you noticed.

Example: I think I'll call this Firefighter "The Angry Outburster."

Firefighter behavior name:

Example: I think I'll call this Firefighter "The Angry Outburster."

- ☐ The Late-Night Snacker
- ☐ The Netflix Marathoner
- ☐ The Social Media Scroller
- ☐ The Sleeper
- ☐ The Online Shopper
- ☐ The Drinker
- ☐ The Ghost (i.e., one who withdraws completely)
- ☐ The Numb Scroller (i.e., jumps from app to app, video to video, completely zoning out)
- ☐ Other: ______________________________

You might have more than one—just notice which ones feel most familiar.

Step 6: Thank your Firefighter part. Before you finish, take a moment to thank your Firefighter part for trying to help you. You might say quietly:

"I see you were trying to keep me safe when I felt hurt."
"Thank you for working so hard to help me not feel so much pain."
"I'm open to learning more about you."

Step 7: Reflect on what you learned. Take a moment to write down:

What surprised you about your Firefighter parts?

Example: I truly never realized how fast they jump in until I did this exercise. It's almost automatic. I also didn't expect to find some sadness underneath the behaviors once I looked closer.

____

____

____

What feels a little clearer now?

Example: In the situation I recalled, I can see that my Firefighter resorted to a bit of anger. Slamming the lid made me feel better. At the same time, it was like a big loud "pause" inside me, like hitting the brakes on something.

____

____

____

____

Exiles: Your Hidden Wounds… And Keeper of Lost Gifts

This is probably as personal as I can get.

One summer, when I was about 8 years old, my family went somewhere for a few days. (I don't recall where.) Mom was visiting a friend, so left to his own devices, my father suddenly announced that he was taking me and my twin brothers to the movies! I was soooo excited.

When we were about to leave, my father saw that I didn't have shoes on. I had blue and white flip-flops. (To this day, I can vividly recall looking down at my flip-flops. Needless to say, I remember every detail of their design.)

Dad: *Oh, Ava, you didn't pack shoes?*
Me: *Ah, I guess not.*
Dad: *You can't come with us today, sweetheart.*

And they left. Just like that.

An older cousin tried to console me, but somehow, the more he tried to pacify me, the more embarrassment and humiliation I felt inside.

I said something like, *"It's probably a lame kiddie movie, anyway,"* and proceeded to do probably one of my best acting performances.

As I grew older, I learned to hide these feelings of "not being good enough," "being left out," and being shamed and abandoned, somewhere deep inside me—like a locked box in the basement of my soul.

And, of course, since I never addressed it, that hurt never went away. It just got buried, and buried. And then some days, the slightest rejection would cause me the deepest pain.

Odd, isn't it? To be deeply hurt, devastated even, by a few minutes of not being chosen, even decades later.

With IFS therapy, I now know that an Exile part was created that day. And I've learned that **Exiles don't grow up just because we do.** They wait. They remember. **And they'll keep hurting—until that moment when "Self" turns toward them with compassion**.

So, Exiles are the parts of you that carry your deepest pain—your shame, your fear, your loneliness. They hold onto the memories and feelings you couldn't handle at the time, because it felt too dangerous or too overwhelming.

Exiles often feel young and very raw. They might be carrying:

- A deep sense of unworthiness or shame.
- Memories of rejection, neglect, or emotional abandonment.
- The heartbreak of a time you were laughed at, dismissed, or left alone.
- The terror of moments when safety or boundaries were violated.
- Burdens of guilt, self-blame, or confusion from experiences of abuse.
- A deep longing to be seen, heard, and protected (because no one was ever there).
- Silent pain from being told (or shown) that your feelings didn't matter.

These parts are called Exiles because they're usually pushed out of your awareness. They're hidden away by your Protectors (Manager and Firefighter parts), who work hard to make sure you don't have to feel those painful memories.

Mind you, it's not that Protectors don't care about your pain. It's the opposite; they care too much. They're afraid that if the Exiles come up, the pain will overwhelm you and that you'll be too hurt to function.

Common Exile Themes

Just like with Managers and Firefighters, Exiles show up in different ways for different people. Here are some common themes of Exile parts you might recognize:

- **The Lonely Child** – The part that feels alone or unloved.
- **The Ashamed One** – The part that carries deep feelings of shame or not being good enough. It often holds the belief, *"I'm fundamentally flawed,"* and hides to avoid being exposed or judged.
- **The Rejected or Abandoned One** – The part that remembers times you felt excluded or dismissed.
- **The Scared One** – The part that holds memories of fear, anxiety, or trauma.
- **The Sad (or Grieving) One**– The part that carries deep sorrow, grief, heartbreak, or loss.
- **The Helpless One** – The part that felt powerless to stop something painful.

You might have one Exile that feels especially strong, or you might notice different Exiles showing up at different times. That's okay; that's normal.

Just remember that in whatever theme they appear, they're always holding something tender—something that's asking for your care and compassion.

Why Exiles Hold the Key to Healing

Even though Exiles can feel overwhelming, it's vital to get to know them and understanding their *whys* for the following reasons:

#1. Exiles quietly shape your present. They're often the reason behind:

- Overreactions that surprise you
- Emotional shutdowns or withdrawal
- Persistent self-doubt or low self-esteem
- Relationship struggles or self-sabotaging habits
- Firefighter behaviors like binge-watching, overeating, or lashing out

These aren't random; they're protective responses trying to shield you from the pain of an Exile being reactivated.

Bottom line: Exiles may be quiet or buried deep down, but they never stop influencing your emotions and behavior.

#2. Exiles can make you feel "stuck" or "emotionally frozen. They carry your deepest pain and unresolved traumas. They carry burdens like: *"I'm not enough," "It was my fault," "I don't matter," "I'm less,"* and many others.

And until those parts are met, understood and handled with compassion and care, you may feel stuck in life. Why? Because the same triggers will keep activating your system in the same old ways.

#3. Exiles hold your lost gifts. Here's something surprising (and truly one of my most cherished learnings from IFS work): the parts of you that were exiled due to pain often carry your most beautiful, essential qualities.

Maybe the part of you that once loved to dance freely shut down after being laughed at.
Maybe your creativity got buried when someone "joked" that your ideas "sucked."
Maybe your deep sensitivity, your ability to feel what others feel, got locked away because it wasn't safe to care that deeply.
Or maybe you're like me, I lost my ability to believe—truly believe—people when they complement me because deep down I was always afraid to get my hopes up.

These qualities don't disappear. They just go underground. And when your Exile parts are finally unburdened, those lost gifts begin to return—not as wounds, but as strengths.

#4. Exiles are the doorway to internal peace. When Exiles are in pain, your Protectors have to stay on constant duty—managing, controlling, distracting, fixing, or numbing.

But once Exiles are unburdened, the entire system relaxes, softens. And there's more space for **Self** to lead.

So what does healing of Exiles actually look like? In IFS, healing an Exile is a gentle, layered process that's led by your **Self**.

- You begin by building trust with your Protectors (Managers and Firefighters), realizing that they're not the enemy. They're just doing their best to keep you safe.
- Next, from a place of Self-energy, you approach the Exile—not to fix it, but to understand it.
- You (Self) witness its pain, let it be heard, and support it in releasing the burdens it's carried for so long.
- And finally, you invite that part back into your internal family system—not as a wound, but as a resource capable of contributing its previously lost gifts (rather than its pain).

Important: As you can deduce from the above gentle and layered process, it's crucial that you strengthen your identity of **Self**.

Why? Because **Self is the only part of you that can do the healing**. Protectors can't heal Exiles; they can only safeguard or suppress them. And your Exiles can't heal themselves; they're still stuck in the pain of past.

Only **Self**—the calm, compassionate, curious presence at your core—has the qualities needed to witness pain without becoming overwhelmed, and to lead the system with clarity and care.

The more connected you are to your **Self-energy**, the more your parts will begin to trust you. That trust is what allows Protectors to soften and Exiles to come forward. Without that solid sense of Self, the healing process can stall or even re-traumatize you by pushing too far, too fast.

So strengthening your identity of Self isn't a nice extra. It's the foundation.

Worksheet 6: Gently Meeting Your Exiles

This exercise will help you start to notice your Exile parts in a way that feels safe and gentle.

Important: There's absolutely no need to heal or unburden your Exiles with this exercise—that comes later. Right now, we're just getting curious.

Think of this like walking through a hallway in your inner world and noticing that one door is closed and locked. You're not barging in. You're simply acknowledging that there's a part of you behind it, waiting.

Important Safety Note

It's okay if you don't feel ready to meet Exiles right now. And if you feel overwhelmed or emotionally flooded at any point, **pause**. Take a few deep breaths, try a grounding practice, or go ahead and focus on the **Self** chapters first. This is *not* a test. Go at your own pace.

Part 1: Just Notice

Think of a time when you felt something or experienced an emotion that seemed *way bigger* than the situation seemed to call for. It could be sadness, shame, rage, rejection, or fear...

anything that hit you harder than expected. **Important:** Don't analyze; just notice.

What happened?

Example: My husband and I were in the car and I mentioned something like having a craving for ice cream because it was so hot. He said something like, "Too late! We already passed the supermarket." And just like that, I felt dismissed. My thoughts ran wildly, thinking, "Why is it that when I want something, NOBODY cares or makes an effort."

____

____

____

____

____

How did you feel in your body?

Example: I had a tightness in my chest, and I felt like crying.

____

____

____

____

____

How "old" did that feeling feel? *(i.e., does this feeling carry the weight of something you've felt for a long time—maybe even since childhood, or is it a recent feeling?)*

Example: Wow. Old. Very old.

____

____

____

____

____

What other thoughts, if any, came up in your mind?

Example: I started to list in my head ALL the things I do for my husband without being asked. When I'm like this (because this isn't the first time I felt this way) I start to wonder how it would be married to someone else.

____

____

____

____

____

Next, imagine that there's a younger part of you holding that emotional charge. You don't have to "talk" to them or go digging for details. Just ask yourself:

What might this part have experienced that made it feel this way?

Example: Being ignored. Just so many memories of being ignored.

____

____

____

____

____

***What do I sense it might be carrying?* (e.g., fear, shame, grief, loneliness)**

Example: I sense deep loneliness and feeling of "being unseen."

____

____

____

____

____

What does this part believe about me or the world?

Example: I think it believes that no one is here to take care of me in any way.

____

____

____

____

____

If nothing comes, that's okay. Just note what you *do* feel even if it's blankness, numbness, or confusion.

Part 2: Say "Hello" from Self

Now take a moment to check in with your Self. Do you think you you (Self) can send your Exile part a little compassion or curiosity? Just a simple *"It's okay. I see you"* or *"I want to understand you when you're ready"* will do.

How does your body respond when you do that?

Example: I feel less tense on my shoulders and jaw.

____

____

____

____

That's it. You don't have to do anything more with any exiled part today. For now, you've done something powerful just by noticing.

Important: Is there anything you need right now? Some rest, grounding exercise, a short walk in nature, or just a break? If so, then please take the time to go and do it. Showing yourself kindness and compassion is part of the journey.

The Self: Your Calm, Wise Center

Imagine a busy household in the middle of a hectic morning. The kids are arguing, the breakfast plates and cutlery are banging on the table, the dog is barking, the coffee is taking forever to brew, and so on.

In the midst of the noise and confusion, there's a parent who stands calmly in the kitchen. They aren't yelling or getting pulled into the arguments. They're not running from one end of the kitchen to the other either. They're just taking a deep breath, hearing everyone, and thinking, *"I see what's happening. But I don't need to step into anything. I'm fine standing and flipping pancakes right here."*

In IFS, the **Self** is like that calm, wise parent. It's not another part of the chaos—it's the steady center that can hold all the noise and still be gentle, caring, and steady.

Unlike the Managers, Firefighters, or Exiles, the Self isn't trying to control or protect. It's there to **listen**, **understand**, and **lead**.

When your Self is **differentiated** from your parts, it can see each one with kindness. It doesn't judge your Manager for being so controlling or your Firefighter for shutting everything down. It doesn't push your Exiles away for feeling so raw and tender. The Self knows that every part has a story and a reason for showing up—and that all of them deserve to be seen and heard.

("Differentiated" is an IFS term that means your Self is separate from your Protectors and Exile parts, not merged or overwhelmed by them.)

So, one of the first goals of IFS is to strengthen your Self so that it becomes a leader; one capable of connecting with your *parts,* so that the whole inner family heals, feels safer and becomes more balanced.

Worksheet 7: The Lighthouse

In IFS, when you're experiencing internal chaos, lacking clarity, feeling stuck in life, or feeling like there are just too many voices inside you, it usually means that your **Self is blended** or merged with your *parts* (Firefighters, Managers and Exiles).

That is, your *parts* are so strong and loud inside you that **Self** is overwhelmed and drowned out, and as such cannot exert itself as the leader of your internal family.

So, one of the key goals in IFS is that you learn to become **differentiated** (separated, unmerged) from your *parts* so that you can *see* them, *listen* to them, and *lead* them, without becoming *them*.

To help you understand this idea more clearly, let's borrow a concept from **Acceptance and Commitment Therapy (ACT)** called the **Observing Self**.

The **Observing Self** refers to the part of you that is able to simply notice your experiences without getting caught up in them. It's the "You/Self" that is aware of what you're thinking, feeling, and sensing, but is **distinct** from the thoughts and feelings themselves.

In IFS terms, this maps beautifully to the **Self** — the inner leader who is calm, curious, and compassionate.

Applying this to IFS, the goal is to become the Self that is aware of what your Manager, Firefighter, and Exile parts are thinking, feeling, sensing, and reacting to—but you are apart (**differentiated!**) from these parts at the same time. This means you can *relate* to a part, instead of being *taken over* by it.

Without a doubt, being differentiated takes practice.

At this time, you're probably so blended (merged) with your parts that it's hard not to join them and share their thoughts and feelings. But remember, that's not the goal of Self; the goal of self is to be the impartial, but compassionate leader.

So, to help your Self become differentiated from your parts, try this exercise.

Step 1: Get comfortable. Find a quiet space. Sit or lie down with your spine supported. Close your eyes if you feel comfortable doing so. Take a few slow, deep breaths. Let your attention begin to settle inward.

Step 2: Imagine the Lighthouse. Picture a tall, strong lighthouse standing on a rocky shoreline.

The wind is wild. The ocean waves are crashing against the rocks. Storm clouds move across the sky. This weather represents your thoughts, emotions, and parts — all the inner activity that comes and goes.

But the lighthouse doesn't move.

The lighthouse stays steady, anchored because its job isn't to control the storm; it simply shines its light. It observes. It stands watch.

You are the lighthouse.

Step 3: Notice the weather. Now gently bring your awareness to your inner world.

What "weather" is present right now?
Are there stormy waves of anxiety? Heavy clouds of sadness? Sharp winds of anger? Or are the waters calm today?

Just notice. You don't need to fix or change anything. Remind yourself: *"This is the weather. I am not the weather. I am the Lighthouse who notices it."*

Step 4: Close gently. When you're ready, take a few deep breaths. Wiggle your fingers or toes, and then gently bring your awareness back to the room.

Step 5: Reflect. Write down your thoughts on these points:

What did you notice when you imagined yourself as the lighthouse?

Example: It was awkward at first. I couldn't quite sit still for the first minute or two.

____

____

____

____

____

Did you feel more "space" as you tried to think of yourself as the Lighthouse and your emotions as the weather?

Example: Yes, eventually. At first, it was hard to separate the thoughts and feelings from myself. I kept thinking "I'm the one thinking this," or "I'm feeling this, so it must be me." But as I kept returning to the image of the Lighthouse, something softened. I began to notice a bit of space between me and what I was feeling. The "storm" was still there, but I wasn't inside it anymore.

___

___

___

___

___

What surprised you?

Example: Honestly? I was surprised why I've never thought of myself as separate from thoughts and feelings. The more I embraced the Lighthouse metaphor, the more it made sense!

___

___

___

___

___

Worksheet 8: Sensing Your Self

The **Self** can feel like a quiet, steady presence inside you. But even if you can't always feel it right away—it's there. This gentle exercise will help you start to notice your Self more.

Unlike The Lighthouse, which focused on noticing your *parts* (and their thoughts and emotions) from a distance, this exercise helps you connect more deeply with your Self—the calm, steady center behind it all.

Important: Be gentle with yourself. If you're finding it a bit hard to connect with your inner core today, that's okay. There's no rush. Go at your own pace.

Step 1: Find a comfortable space. Sit somewhere calm and safe. Let your body relax and take a few slow, deep breaths.

Step 2: Close your eyes and notice. Gently close your eyes and bring your attention *inward*.

Important: Just notice; there's no need to react, change or fix anything. You're simply trying to become aware of Self.

- Notice anything inside your body right now, like a tight chest, a flutter in your stomach, a lump in your throat, or heaviness in your shoulders.
- Are there any parts that feel loud, tense, or busy? Perhaps a part that's worrying, planning, judging, or trying to make something go away?

Step 3: Invite your Self to be present. In your mind, quietly say something like:

"I'm here."
"I just want to be."
"I give myself the gift of time and quiet."

Optional: Accompany the above thoughts with a physical gesture like putting your right hand on your left shoulder like a half-hug, placing a hand over heart, or gently pressing your fingertips together. Why? This physical gesture activates the **parasympathetic nervous system** (your "rest and digest" or "relaxation" system), which supports the felt sense of Self.[7,8]

Step 4: Notice any shifts. As you say these words, see if you feel even a tiny bit more calm, curious, or open. That gentle, quiet feeling is your Self starting to show up.

Step 5: Slowly end this exercise. When you're ready, slowly open your eyes, take a few deep breaths, or do some light stretching before you go on with your day.

Food for thought: Did you notice that mindfulness and connecting to Self often go hand in hand? Both invite you to slow down, turn inward, and observe without judgment.

In many ways, mindfulness is one of the doorways to Self — a way to create just enough space between you and your parts so you can begin to listen with compassion.

Creating Your IFS Parts Map

Great job exploring the basics of IFS! Now let's bring it all together in a way that's personal and meaningful to you—by creating your own **IFS Parts Map**.

This map is like a gentle sketch or diagram that shows the different parts of you (as you see them now) and how they relate to each other. It's a way to take what's inside and bring it out in a visual, easy-to-see way.

Why do this? Drawing your IFS Parts Map helps you see your inner world in a new light. It's a gentle way to bring more understanding and curiosity to your parts, and to begin recognizing the roles they play in your daily life.

Why do this *now*? I find that it's a great exercise to do before diving deeper into IFS. It's like having a "*before*" snapshot of your internal system, something you can return to later and compare with how your inner relationships evolve over time.

By the way, when you draw your IFS Parts Map, you don't have to be an artist! It's not about making it look perfect; it's about capturing how your parts feel and how they show up for you.

Worksheet 9: Creating Your IFS Parts Map

Step 1: Gather your materials. Find some blank paper, markers, colored pencils, or whatever feels good to you. This is your personal map, so make it as simple or as colorful as you'd like.

Step 2: Begin with your Self. In the center of your page, draw a circle or a symbol to represent your Self—your calm, wise center. Label it "**Self**" so you remember that this is the part of you that can lead with compassion and understanding.

Step 3: Add your parts. Around the Self, start adding circles or shapes for your different parts. If you want, you can draw them out, too. You might have:

- *Manager parts (like the Perfectionist, the Caretaker, or the Inner Critic).*
- *Firefighter parts (like the Overeater, the Social Media Scroller, or the Numb One).*
- *Exile parts (like the Lonely Child, the Ashamed One, or the Scared One).*

Label each part in a way that feels true for you. If you're not sure what to name them yet, just write how they feel—like *"The part that worries all the time,"* or *"The one that wants to disappear,"* or *"The one that gets tense and panicky at the slightest change of plans,"* etc.

Step 4: Notice relationships. Draw lines or arrows between parts if you notice how they interact. For example, maybe your Inner Critic Manager is always watching over your Scared Exile, or your Firefighter part jumps in whenever your Exile part's pain comes up.

Gentle reminder: This isn't about getting it perfect or creating a work of art. You're just trying to notice how your parts might relate to each other.

Step 5: Add gentle words of care. Before you finish, take a moment to write one kind word or phrase for your whole system. Something like:

"I see all of you."
"You're trying to help in your own ways."
"We're all here together."

Following is the IFS Parts Map I first drew when I started my IFS therapy journey. *(I originally sketched this out on paper, but I re-created it in Canva so I could share it with you here.)*

I knew I tended to overthink things, so when I created my IFS parts map, I wanted to simply write down what came to my mind. *(I didn't want to "analyze" my thoughts.)*

Some of my realizations:

- I found "Self" the hardest to map. I truly couldn't visualize myself at the time, so I just put the word in the middle.
- My Exile part (*The Invisible One*) was the next one I drew, and she came pretty quickly to me. Before I learned IFS, I had already gone through other therapies (DBT and ACT), so I had a good idea of my inner child and her sensitivities.
- I then named my Manager part (*The Overachiever*), and she came to me pretty quickly, too.
- Next, I drew my Firefighter part, which I eventually called *Ms. Up and Down*. This one took some thinking, which is why I drew it smaller than my Manager part.
- Lastly, I wrote down words of kindness to myself at the corner.

To be honest, I was surprised at how much time I spent thinking about my Self. I didn't realize that my concept of Self was still so vague then.

I also noticed that my Protector parts were almost "not on speaking terms" with each other. They were both focused heavily on my Exile part. And since it took me a while to draw my Firefighter, I realized afterward that my Manager part was the more dominant one.

Now, remember, your parts map doesn't need to look like mine. Simply taking the time to create it is already an act of care for yourself.

When you're done, take a moment to look at your map — and then gently put it away.

Why? Because looking at your IFS Parts Map can be emotionally activating. It's important to see your parts and honor their presence, but you don't want to linger too long or start analyzing everything at once.

Putting the map away signals to your system that there's no rush. You're approaching this work at a calm, steady pace. It models healthy internal boundaries and helps your Self and your parts feel safe and not overwhelmed.

Strengthening Self: Awaken Your Inner Hero

"Within you, there is a stillness and a sanctuary to which you can retreat at any time and be yourself."
– Hermann Hesse

Strengthening the Self is the key to everything. This is central to the entire IFS model.

- **Self is the healing agent in IFS**.

Managers, Firefighters, and even Exiles cannot heal themselves. They're too burdened or protective. Plus, it's not their role to lead. Their job is to respond to pain (or try to prevent it), not to lead the system.

Healing only happens when Self is present with its natural qualities: *compassion, curiosity, calm, courage, clarity, confidence, creativity,* and *connectedness.*

- **Self leads the internal system.**

The goal of IFS isn't to eliminate parts. It's to help your parts trust **Self** enough to step back and let it lead. When Self is strong, your inner world becomes more cooperative, balanced, and peaceful.

Without Self, you stay blended.

If Self is weak, inaccessible, or unavailable, it's more likely to be blended (fused, merged) with your parts. So if parts are overwhelmed by anxiety, rage, shame, numbness, perfectionism, or people-pleasing, so is Self. And when Self is blended, it's unable to see the bigger picture.

So, before you can truly connect with and care for your parts, you need a solid foundation inside.

How can your Self become the steady leader of your inner family? You must awaken the strength that's already inside you—the part of you that can say:

I am here.
I am listening.
I can help.
I am your safe space.
You don't have to do this alone anymore.

This whole chapter is dedicated to helping you find and strengthen your Self, and **reclaim** your role as the compassionate leader of your inner world.

The 8 Cs of Self-Energy

You can't pour from an empty cup.
You can't give what you don't have.
You must tend to your own fire before you can light the way for others.

We've all heard versions of these phrases before, and they all point to the same truth: **You must take care of your Self before you can truly care for others.** Not just physically, but emotionally, mentally, and energetically.

In IFS, this doesn't mean self-care in the bubble bath or journaling sense (though those help, too!). It means learning to **lead from Self-energy.**

And how do you cultivate this Self-energy? By developing and nurturing the following qualities.

CALMNESS: A sense of steadiness, even when things feel big or messy.

Why? Because calmness helps you stay grounded and present, preventing you from being swept up by inner and outer chaos.

How?

- Take a few slow, steady breaths when you feel overwhelmed.
- Notice where in your body you feel tension, and see if you can gently soften it.
- Spend a few quiet moments in nature or somewhere peaceful to help your nervous system settle.
- Something to do today/this week: Set aside 5 minutes each morning for quiet breathing. No phone, no agenda—just notice your breath and let your nervous system settle before the day begins.

CURIOSITY: Interest to learn about what's really going on—without judgment.

Why? Because curiosity opens the door to understanding, instead of reacting or avoiding.

How?

- Instead of thinking *"What's wrong?"* try asking, *"I wonder what's going on?"*
- Treat thoughts, feelings, and situations as puzzles to be explored, not as problems to be fixed.
- Remember this: If you don't know for sure, you're just guessing.

- Something to do today/this week: Do something *unfamiliar* (e.g., read up on a new topic or try out a hobby you've never done before, etc.) to spark fresh curiosity.

CLARITY: Seeing what's happening without confusion or distortion.

Why? Because clarity lets you recognize what's REAL.

How?

- Practice mindfulness to give yourself that "mental pause" to think things through.
- Write in a journal to sort out your thoughts and feelings.
- When you feel confused, pause and ask, *"What am I really feeling?"*
- Something to do today/this week: Pick one situation that feels confusing and journal about it. Write down what actually happened (facts), what you felt, and what you assumed. Often, separating these (facts, vs. feelings and assumptions) clarifies the picture.

COMPASSION: Extending warmth and understanding toward your own experience.

Why? Because compassion creates a safe space within you.

How?

- Imagine how you would talk to a dear friend, and offer yourself the same warmth.
- Practice self-forgiveness. Acknowledge past errors, and then let them go. Focus on what you *learned* from those experiences, not on replaying the regret.
- Something to do now: Put a hand on your heart and say something kind to yourself, like *"I'm doing the best I can."*

<u>CONFIDENCE</u>: A quiet sense of inner knowing: *"I can handle this."*

Why? Because confidence keeps you steady even when emotions rise.

How?

- Remind yourself of times you've gotten through hard things in the past.
- Say to yourself, *"I can handle this, one step at a time."*
- Notice the small ways you're already showing up with strength each day.
- Something to do today/this week: Identify one small task you've been avoiding and complete it this week—then pause to acknowledge it: "*I did that.*" Build trust with yourself through follow-through.

COURAGE: The willingness to face what's there (pain, truth, vulnerability), even if it feels a little scary.

Why? Because healing requires presence, and presence requires bravery.

How?

- Celebrate little acts of bravery, like speaking your truth or sitting with a tough feeling.
- Take small steps to face feelings or memories that scare you, rather than forcing yourself to confront them all at once.
- Set clear boundaries to protect your energy and safety. Courage isn't about pushing past your limits; it's about honoring them.
- Something to do today/this week: Share one honest thought or feeling with someone you trust, even if it feels vulnerable. (It doesn't have to be huge—just more real than you usually would be.)

CREATIVITY: The ability to think outside the box, focus on possibilities (not limits), and find new solutions to old problems.

Why? Because creativity brings fresh perspective and flexibility, preventing getting stuck in old, unhelpful patterns.

How?

- Try approaching a familiar challenge from a completely different angle. Ask yourself, *"What if I did the opposite of my usual response?"*
- Expose yourself to new ideas, environments, and people to spark inspiration and shift your perspective.
- Something to do today/this week: Do something playful for 20 minutes this week like doodling, writing, cooking, etc.—any activity where you can freely express yourself without needing it to be perfect.

CONNECTEDNESS: A feeling of being in a meaningful relationship with yourself and the world around you. It's a sense of belonging and harmony.

Why? Humans are social creatures; we're not meant to be alone.[9,10] When you feel connected—both to your inner Self and to the people and environments that matter to you—you experience a deeper sense of safety, purpose, and support.

How?

- Make time to connect with people you trust and feel safe with, even if it's just a quick text, call, or shared silence.
- Spend time in nature to remind yourself you're part of something larger—notice the seasons, sounds, and rhythms around you.

- Practice connecting inward by checking in with yourself regularly: *"How am I feeling right now? What do I need?"*
- Something to do today/this week: Reach out to one person you care about (friend, family, or colleague) just to check in, with no agenda.

You don't need to develop the above qualities from scratch. It is generally believed that these qualities are inherent to all human beings. You just need to decide to develop them further.

Just choose one or two that feel most natural to you right now, and explore them gently. Over time, and with continuous practice, you'll see how these Self qualities grow stronger and bring more balance and healing to your inner family.

Wise Mind (from DBT)

In addition to the 8 Cs of Self-Energy, there's another principle that can help you *access* your calm, centered place: **Wise Mind**.

This concept comes from Dialectical Behavior Therapy (DBT). It describes a balanced way of responding to life, one where emotions and logic work *together* instead of fighting for control.

Emotion Mind is when you're swept up entirely in feelings—anxious, angry, or overwhelmed. Everything feels urgent, and it's hard to see the big picture.

Reasonable Mind is when you're focused only on facts and logic, shutting out your emotions. It can be rigid, over-analytical, or disconnected.

Wise Mind is when you can hold both. You feel your emotions *and* think clearly at the same time.

Important: This does NOT mean that your Self is composed of two parts (Reasonable Mind and Emotion Mind). **Self is who you are. Wise Mind is a skill** that can help you access Self.

Why This Matters in IFS

Wise Mind helps you **pause and step back** from being completely swept up in either emotional intensity or cold logic.

In IFS terms, this practice can be a **pathway into Self-energy** because it gently *unblends* you from purely emotional parts (often Exiles or Firefighters) or purely logical (often Managers), making you capable of accessing the steady, compassionate leader within.

Over time, using Wise Mind builds trust between your parts and your Self because they feel heard, respected, and guided—not pushed aside or ignored.

Again, think of Self as the calm, compassionate parent of your internal family. When your Protectors and Exiles see that you can truly listen to all of them and respond with balanced, thoughtful leadership, their trust in you grows.

And the more they trust your Self to lead, the less they'll feel the need to take over.

Worksheet 10: Wise Mind

Here's how you can quickly practice Wise Mind in your daily life.

Step 1: Find a quiet space. Sit somewhere comfortable and take a few slow, steady breaths. Let your body settle. Remind yourself that there's no rush.

Step 2: Ask. Take a deep breath, put a hand on your heart, and gently ask:

What do I know in my heart right now?

Example: I know that I'm tired, and there's a sadness inside me I can't explain.

____

____

____

____

What do I know in my head?

Example: I know that I have a lot on my plate, and I've been skipping rest and self-care because I keep telling myself I don't have time.

____

____

____

____

Step 3: Bring them together. Imagine an inner meeting place where your feelings and your thoughts sit together at the same table. What would happen if they listened to each other with kindness?

What does my Wise Mind say when I hold both truths?

Example: I need to take an evening off this week, even if it means leaving some tasks unfinished. My health and well-being are worth protecting.

____

____

____

____

Tip: Use this exercise whenever you feel overwhelmed or unsure about a decision. If you can't get to a quiet spot, simply close your eyes for a moment and ask yourself the questions above in a gentle, quiet way.

Values Clarification (from ACT)

What makes you happy?
What kind of person do you want to be?
What are your values?

The above questions might seem simple, but they stop most people in their tracks. Ask someone what they want, and they quickly answer "to be happy." Ask them what *exactly* makes them happy, and they're stumped for words.

I know because I used to be like this.

I realized that it was hard for me to move forward and heal because I had no idea what direction I wanted to go. Even my values were a bit tangled. I valued honesty—who doesn't? But as a chronic people-pleaser, my "honesty" usually meant I told others what *they* wanted to hear. I was betraying myself every time I silenced my own truth to keep the peace.

That's when I learned something crucial: to truly connect with my Self, I needed to define my core values first. *(Values Clarification is a core skill in Acceptance and Commitment Therapy (ACT), and it can be a powerful tool in IFS, too.)*

Values are the things that matter most to you in your life. They're like a compass that points you in the direction you want to go, even when things feel messy or hard.

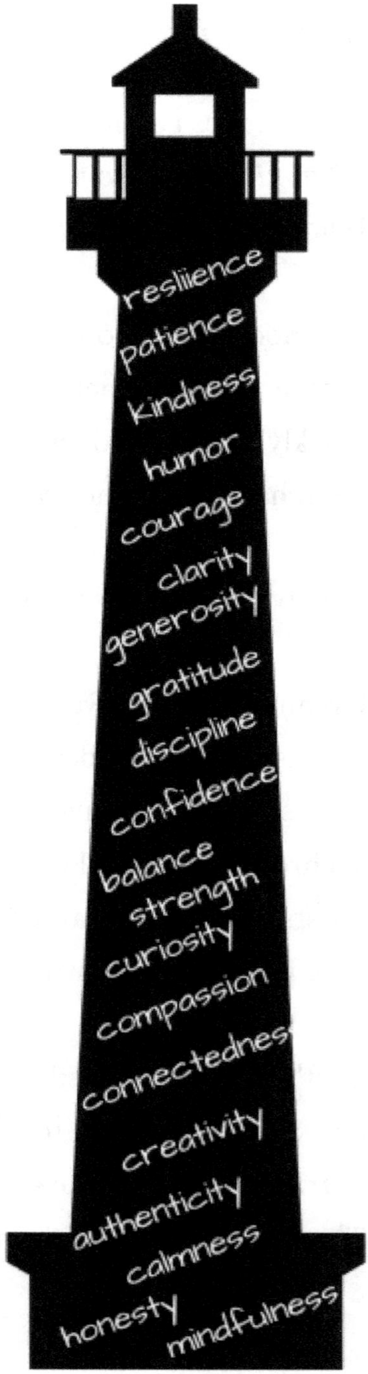

Values aren't about what you "should" do or what other people or society expect from you. They're about what feels deeply true and important to **you**. They're the qualities and principles that make you feel most alive, most connected, and most like yourself.

Why This Matters in IFS

When you're working with your parts, it's easy to get lost in *their* worries and fears. But your values are like a steady light in the background. They remind your Self that even when your parts are scared or loud, you have a bigger vision guiding you forward.

Remember The Lighthouse exercise?

Imagine the light of that lighthouse being powered by your core values. *(Note that the core values in the Lighthouse include the 8 C's of Energy.)*

Bottom line: When you're clear about your values, it's easier to make choices that truly fit you (or who you want to be)—even when different parts of you have strong and conflicting opinions, and fears.

Worksheet 11: Clarifying Your Values

This exercise aims to help you take a step back and re-evaluate the values that matter most to you, and use them to guide your Self-leadership.

Step 1: Name your core values. Write down up to 10 values from the list below that feel most important to you. *(Feel free to add your own if something isn't listed.)*

Example values: Authenticity, Growth, Adventure, Love, Health, Honesty, Compassion, Learning, Creativity, Freedom, Kindness, Connection, Family, Integrity, Playfulness, Spirituality, Justice, Peace, Humor, Courage, Calmness, Curiosity, Clarity, Confidence, Mindfulness, Leadership, Loyalty, Generosity.

List your Top 10 Values:

1.) ______________________________

2.) ______________________________

3.) ______________________________

4.) ______________________________

5.) ______________________________

6.) ______________________________

7.) ______________________________

8.) ______________________________

9.) ______________________________

10.) ____________________________

Step 2: Narrow it down. From your list of 10, choose the Top 5 values that feel most central to who you want to be and how you want to live.

Your Top 5 Values:

1.) ____________________________
2.) ____________________________
3.) ____________________________
4.) ____________________________
5.) ____________________________

Step 3: Define them in your own words. For each of your top 5 values, write what it means to YOU, not what it means to other people.

Example: "Creativity" to me means ***making time*** *for my passion. I'm an accountant but I like to cook and experiment with different cuisines. So creativity for me means taking the time to indulge this hobby.*

____

____

____

____

____

____

____

____

____

____

Step 4: Connect to Self. For each value, ask yourself:

How does this value make me feel when I'm living it?

Example: When I practice my creativity in the kitchen, I feel... free. No pressure whatsoever; no deadline to meet, no expected result to achieve.

____

____

____

____

____

How does this value manifest in my body when I'm living it?

Example: I feel energized in my chest, like I'm buzzing with giddiness.

____

____

____

____

____

Step 5: Put it into action. Choose one value and list two small ways you can live it this week.

Value:

Example: Mindfulness

____

Action 1:

Example: Spend 10 minutes each morning just being quiet.

____

____

Action 2:

Example: Walk outdoors in nature alone at least twice this week.

____

____

Worksheet 12: Values Compass

This exercise will help you visualize your values as the guiding points that help your **Self** navigate your inner family.

Step 1: Core value. Write your main guiding value in the center of the compass below. Choose the one that feels like the heartbeat of your life.

Step 2: Additional values. Place four other important values on the four compass points: North, East, South, and West. Here's an example:

Step 3: Live according to your values. As you move through your week, imagine your **Self** standing at the center, using these values to guide your actions and choices.

How to apply this in IFS practice:

- When a Protector (Manager or Firefighter part) tries to take over, pause and imagine looking at your compass.
- Ask: *If I choose in line with my North Star value right now, what would I do?*
- Let your Self and your values (not the parts) steer your actions.

Here's an example situation: You've had a very stressful day and you're feeling down. A Firefighter part jumps in with a strong urge to binge on snacks and zone out in front of the TV.

- **Center (Confidence):** From Self-energy, remind your parts, *"We can handle this."* Confidence here is your Self reassuring the Firefighter that you're capable of meeting and handling the days stress and pressures.

- **North (Leadership):** Self steps into the role of leader. Instead of letting the Firefighter run the show, you thank it for wanting to help, and let it know you'll consider its needs along with the needs of the rest of your system. Imagine saying, *"I hear you and I know you want to help. Let's take a pause and evaluate what's best."*

- **East (Loyalty):** Your Self shows loyalty to *all* your parts, including your future self. This might mean finding a way to soothe and comfort the Firefighter while staying loyal to your body's health.

- **South (Empathy):** Self listens with compassion: *"I get it. It's been a hard day, and food feels comforting."* By showing empathy, the Firefighter feels seen and may soften its urgency (i.e., that burning feeling to binge eat)

- **West (Honesty):** Self gently brings truth into the conversation: *"We both know that binging only provides temporary relief. And that we tend to feel worse afterwards because we feel like we betrayed out health goals."* Important: This isn't shaming. It's clarity offered from a caring place.

Outcome: Instead of suppressing or giving in automatically, your Self listens, validates, and works with the Firefighter to find a choice that meets its need for comfort without harming the system—maybe a smaller snack, a warm drink, or another soothing activity.

Your turn to create your Values Compass now:

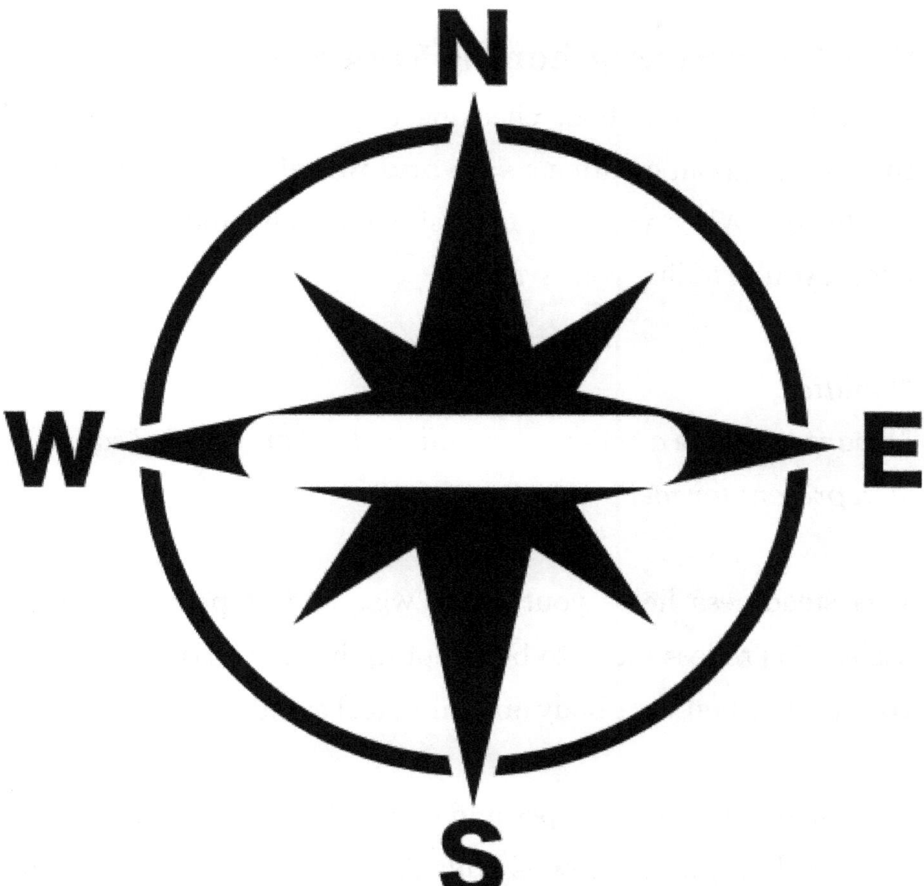

Self-Care + Self-Compassion

To nurture and strengthen your sense of Self, it's essential to practice both self-care and self-compassion.

Self-Care: Strengthening Your Self

Self-care isn't just about checking off a to-do list of "healthy" things—it's about creating a **safe and nourishing foundation** inside you. When you rest, nourish your body, and tend to your needs, you're telling your system:

"I matter."
"I want to create a space where all parts of me can feel safe."
"I'm present for me."

This steadiness helps your calm, wise Self step forward more easily. You're less likely to be swept up in the worries or fears of your parts when your body and mind feel cared for and balanced.

Self-care comes in all shapes and sizes—think of it like a personal treasure hunt, and below is your list of "finds." See how many you can check off in a week!

☐ Take a short walk in nature—listen to the birds and feel the fresh air on your skin.

- ☐ Make yourself a cup of tea or coffee and take at least five minutes to really savor the warmth.
- ☐ Take a warm bath or shower. Imagine the water washing away stress.
- ☐ Curl up with a cozy blanket and read a book that comforts or inspires you.
- ☐ Write in a journal. Just let your thoughts and feelings flow.
- ☐ Light a candle and sit quietly for a few moments of calm.
- ☐ Listen to music that lifts your spirit or soothes your soul.
- ☐ Try some gentle stretches or yoga to help your body feel more open.
- ☐ Give yourself a little hand or foot massage with lotion or oil.
- ☐ Prepare a meal that feels nourishing and grounding.
- ☐ Do a short meditation or breathing exercise—just a few minutes of stillness.
- ☐ Watch a funny or feel-good movie to let yourself laugh and relax.
- ☐ Spend time with a pet or loved one who makes you feel safe and calm.
- ☐ Sit outside and watch the clouds drift by or the sun set.
- ☐ Color in a coloring book or doodle—no pressure to make it perfect!
- ☐ Write a letter of kindness to yourself.
- ☐ Take a break from social media or your phone for a little while.
- ☐ Write at least three things for which you're grateful.

- ☐ Wear something soft and comfortable—clothes that feel like a hug.
- ☐ Try a new creative activity—painting, crafting, music, baking, gardening—just for fun.
- ☐ Take a nap—give yourself permission to rest.
- ☐ Go to bed a little earlier than usual.
- ☐ Get out of bed a little later than usual.
- ☐ Let yourself daydream about something that brings you hope.
- ☐ Gently put a hand on your heart and say, *"I'm here. I care for myself."*

Self-Compassion: How You Relate to Yourself

Self-compassion is the **attitude** you bring to your self-care and your healing journey. It's about how you talk to yourself when things are hard, and how you hold your pain and your parts with warmth.

Here's your self-compassion checklist. Choose one that feels right for you and say it to yourself whenever you need comfort.

- ☐ I'm doing the best I can, and that's enough.
- ☐ It's okay to not have it all figured out.
- ☐ I'm allowed to take things one step at a time.
- ☐ I deserve kindness, especially from myself.
- ☐ My feelings matter, even if they're hard to hold.
- ☐ I'm allowed to rest and care for myself.

- ☐ I don't have to be perfect to be worthy of love.
- ☐ I see how hard I'm trying, and I honor that effort.
- ☐ I can be gentle with myself, even when I make mistakes.
- ☐ I trust that I'm growing in my own time and way.
- ☐ I forgive myself for the ways I've struggled to cope.
- ☐ I deserve compassion, no matter what's going on.
- ☐ I'm allowed to feel what I feel without judgment.
- ☐ I'm learning to be kind to the parts of me that hurt.
- ☐ I honor the small wins and the little steps I take.
- ☐ I'm not alone—others feel this way too.
- ☐ My worth isn't measured by what I do—it's in who I am.
- ☐ I'm grateful for the strength it takes to keep going.
- ☐ I'm learning to trust my own inner wisdom.
- ☐ My struggles don't define me; my courage does.
- ☐ I'm proud of myself for showing up today.
- ☐ I offer myself the same love I would give a dear friend.
- ☐ It's okay to have hard days—healing is not a straight line.
- ☐ I choose to treat myself with patience and respect.
- ☐ I'm here for myself, no matter what.

Self-care and self-compassion work together. Self-care helps your body and mind feel **safe**—like building a cozy home for your parts. Self-compassion helps you create a sense of **warmth** and **acceptance** in that home, no matter what parts are feeling. Neither is about perfection—it's about creating a daily practice of meeting yourself with kindness.

Cultivating Self-Leadership Daily

You've been neglecting yourself for a long time. As such, strengthening your connection to the Self isn't something that happens all at once—it's a gentle, ongoing practice. Just like you might water a plant each day, you can water the calm, wise energy of your Self by weaving small practices into your daily life.

Here are a few simple ways to help you feel more connected to your Self every day. **Tip:** Set a soft reminder or alarm so these practices slowly weave into your routine.

Morning Self-Check-Ins. Start your day by taking a few moments to tune into yourself. Before you jump into work, family, or tasks, pause and ask:

"How am I feeling right now?"
"Are there any parts of me that feel loud or worried this morning?"
"What do I need to feel a little more calm and centered?"

This doesn't have to take long—just a minute or two to help your Self gently show up and lead the way.

Mindfulness Practices. Mindfulness is a simple but powerful way to reconnect with your Self throughout the day. You can practice mindfulness in small ways, like:

Taking a few slow breaths when you feel tense.
Noticing the sounds and sights around you with curiosity.
Letting yourself pause and check in with your body—asking, "What's here right now?"

Mindfulness isn't about doing it "perfectly." It's about creating little pauses of presence and care, so your calm, wise Self can guide you more often.

Evening Reflections. At the end of your day, take a quiet moment to reflect. You might write in a journal or simply pause and notice:

"What parts of me showed up today?"
"Did I notice moments when my Self felt calm and clear?"
"Is there anything I'd like to offer myself or my parts as comfort tonight?"

These small practices might not feel like much at first, but they add up. Over time, they help you build a stronger connection to your Self—and that's the foundation for everything else in your IFS journey.

Befriending and Healing Your Parts

> *"I've found that healing begins when my inner world feels balanced, when I no longer fight or contradict myself, and when I can speak in one authentic voice."*
>
> *— Ava Walters*

Before you begin the work of building trust with your parts, take a moment to acknowledge the ground you've already covered—the previous Self chapter!

That's the essential first step—finding and strengthening your center. Without it, trust-building with your parts becomes shaky, like trying to build a bridge without solid supports.

If feel your sense of Self isn't steady yet, there's no rush. Go back, revisit those exercises, and return here when you can stand in your Self with confidence.

And if you're ready—congratulations! You're about to take the next step toward deeper healing.

Building Trust with Your Parts

When you first start noticing and listening to your parts, you might find that they're a little hesitant or unsure to come forward. Imagine sitting quietly and trying to ask your parts *"How are you feeling?"* and you're drawing blanks. This is normal.

Remember, your Managers and Firefighters have been working hard to keep you safe for a long time on their own, and your Exiles have been in the background for so long that they might not be used to someone asking about them.

Imagine hearing from a long-lost relative. At first, you're just confused to hear from them, right?

Building trust is a gentle, patient process. It's about showing your parts, over and over, that you're not here to judge them or push them away. You're here to understand them, to see them, and to help them feel safe enough to be themselves not just today but from now on.

So, **how do you start the process of building trust with your parts**? It starts with the 6 F's in IFS.

The 6 Fs in IFS

The 6 Fs are a simple, structured way to meet and understand your parts—especially when you're just starting out. Think of them as a gentle guide to help you stay connected to your calm, wise Self while you learn about each part's feelings and fears.

Important: Don't rush this process or try to get it perfect—just bring a little curiosity and care.

1. Find. The first step is to **notice** when a part is showing up. This can be something physical (e.g., a tightness in your chest), an emotion (e.g., sudden fear), a thought (e.g., a critical voice in your mind), or even an image (e.g., a very old pair of glasses you lost).

When this happens, simply pause and say to yourself, *"There's a part here."*

2. Focus. Next, gently bring your attention to that part. You might close your eyes, take a slow breath, and really let yourself **feel** where and how the part is manifesting.

For example, if you're feeling the hairs at the back of your neck rise, don't push it away. Spend time with it and observe it with curiosity rather than judgment.

3. Flesh out. Start to explore what the part is feeling or trying to tell you. You might ask:

- *What are you trying to tell me?*
- *What emotions are you holding?*
- *Do you have any images or memories you want me to see?*
- *How do you feel in my body right now?*

Note: You don't have to dive too deep—just let the part show you what it wants you to notice.

4. Feel Toward. Notice how your **Self** feels toward this part. Do you feel curious? Annoyed? Scared? Loving? This is important because it helps you see if you're in your calm, wise Self—or if another part has jumped in. If you feel calm and curious, great! If not, that's okay—just notice.

5. Befriend. Start to build a gentle connection. Let the part know you see it and you're here to listen. For example, suppose it's 10 PM, and a Manager part is pushing you to re-evaluate your 50-page report, you might want to say...

"Thank you, Perfectionist, for showing you care about my presentation on Friday. I understand that you want to make sure it's the very best it can be, and that you're trying to protect

me from mistakes or embarrassment. I appreciate your effort, and I promise we can review it again—just not tonight."

Food for thought: Did you notice the tone Self used in this example? It isn't dismissive; it's calm, caring, and confident. That's the result of cultivating Self-energy!

6. Fear. Finally, gently ask the part: *"What are you afraid would happen if you didn't do what you're doing?"*

Parts often have important fears driving their behavior—like fear of rejection, fear of feeling pain, fear of abandonment, fear of failure, etc.. By asking this question, you're helping the part feel safe enough to share what's really going on underneath.

The 6 Fs are an important part of IFS work because they help you slow down the process of meeting and getting to know your parts.

Going back to our long-lost relative analogy, how would you feel if they tried to bulldoze their way into your world? Not ideal, to say the least. But if they keep showing up and gently making contact—listening to you, respecting your pace, and showing genuine care—you'd probably start to feel safer and more open to connection. It's the same with your parts.

Unblending from Your Parts

In IFS, being **blended** means that a part has stepped in so strongly that it's hard to tell where it ends and your calm, wise Self begins. It's like the part has slid into the driver's seat and your Self is just along for the ride.

When people hear this for the first time, they shake their heads and go, *"Nah, how can I not be in control of myself?!"*

But then again, can you relate to any of these?

- You snap at your partner over something small and feel *nothing* but the heat of anger in that moment.
  *This could be **The Defender** (Manager) stepping in to protect you by pushing others away.*

- You're lying in bed replaying a mistake from work over and over in your head. The anxiety is so loud you can't sleep. Before you know it, it's 4 AM.
  *This could be **The Worrier** (*Manager*) believing that constant vigilance will prevent mistakes or danger.*

- You step on the scale, cringe at what you see, and feel deeply ashamed of yourself.

This could be ***The Shamed One*** *(*Exile*) who carries old feelings of unworthiness and rejection.*

- You avoid opening an email because you're convinced it contains bad news—even though you have no proof.
  This could be ***The Avoider*** *(*Manager*) trying to protect you from disappointment or overwhelm.*

- You spend hours scrolling on your phone to numb out, then realize you don't remember half of what you saw. *This could be* ***The Numb Scroller*** *(Firefighter) distracting you from uncomfortable emotions by shutting them down.*

- You're on your way home and see you partner having lunch with a colleague of the opposite sex. You reach home full of suspicion and self-doubt. You're swinging wildly between *"They're cheating!"* and thoughts of you're not enough.

  These could be ***The Suspicious One*** *(Manager) who scans for threats to protect you from betrayal, and* ***The Insecure One*** *(Manager) who compares you to others to anticipate rejection. Both are often working hard to protect the* ***Unlovable One*** *(Exile) who carries deep fears of not being worthy of love.*

- A coworker makes a sarcastic remark about your work in front of the team. You're fuming inside (or feel shamed) but you force a smile and stay silent. Later, you replay the moment in your mind with all the sharp comebacks you *could have* said.

This could be ***The Peacemaker*** (Manager) *who avoids confrontation or* ***The Suppressed One*** (Manager) *who pushes anger down to prevent conflict. Both are protecting* **The *Powerless One*** (*Exile*) *who holds old experiences of not feeling safe to speak up.*

Does it surprise you to realize that your **Self** may not be leading as much as you thought? It can indeed be shocking at first but know that you are not alone! Many of us live and walk like this every day. Focus and take solaced in the fact that NOW you're doing something about it.

If you don't see yourself in the examples above, note that **blending doesn't have to feel dramatic—it can be subtle**. Here are some gentle signs to watch for:

- **Sudden, overwhelming emotions.** One moment you're okay and then the next a feeling is so strong it takes over. That's usually a sign you're blended with a part.
- **One-track thinking.** If you feel stuck in one story or belief (like *"I'm not good enough"* or *"I know they're going to leave me eventually"),* that's often a part's perspective.

- **Losing your calm, curious Self.** When you feel reactive, defensive, or shut down, it's a sign that a part has stepped in to take charge.
- **Feeling small or childlike.** Sometimes blending feels like being pulled back to an old, familiar feeling from your past—like a small, scared child inside.

Techniques for Unblending

When you're blended with a part, it can feel like you're swept up in a wave of feelings or thoughts, with no clear way to step back. Unblending is the practice of gently creating space between your Self and the part that's taken over—so you can see more clearly and respond with calm and care.

Pause and Breathe

When you notice you're caught in a swirl of painful or unhelpful emotions, pause. Take a few slow, steady breaths. Feel the ground beneath your feet or the chair supporting you. These small pauses remind your system that you don't have to react right away. **Your emotions are valid, but that doesn't mean you need to act on them.**

Name the Part

Say to yourself, *"A part of me is feeling ______________ right now."* This small shift in language—*a part of me*—instead of "I am"—can open up a space for your calm Self to see what's happening.

Check with Your Body

Parts often show up in the body as tightness, heat, coldness, or numbness. When this happens, put a gentle hand on that spot and say, *"I feel you. I'm here to listen."* This physical connection pulls you to the present, instead of getting pulled too deeply into the part's energy.

You can follow this-up with a **soothing touch** like rubbing your hands together, wrapping yourself in a soft blanket, or doing a half-hug. These practices can help your nervous system calm down, creating more space for your Self to step in.

Ask: Who's Here Right Now?

When you feel overwhelmed, gently ask, *"Who's here right now? Is this a part of me, or is this my calm, wise Self?"* This question can help you notice whether you're merged with a part or able to observe it with curiosity.

Visualize Separation

Imagine the part that's loud or scared as a separate figure sitting next to you, rather than inside you. You might picture it as a younger version of you, a shape, or even an image that feels right.

Letting it sit beside you can remind you that it's not all of who you are—it's just one part of you.

Tracking Shifts in Your System

As you practice unblending and getting to know your parts, you might start to notice subtle changes in how you feel inside. These shifts are important clues that your inner family is starting to trust your Self.

Shifts can be big "Aha!" moments or small and gentle changes. They might show up as:

- A sudden sense of calm or relief in your body.
- A part that once felt loud and overwhelming becoming quieter or more open.
- A new feeling of curiosity or compassion where there used to be fear or criticism.
- Noticing a part's voice in a softer or less intense way.
- Feeling less tense or overwhelming emotions over the same trigger(s).

Tracking shifts is a great way to see how far your parts are learning to trust your Self to lead.

Worksheet 13: Shifts Tracker

This worksheet will help you gently notice the small (and sometimes big!) ways your parts and your Self are learning to trust each other more.

Step 1: Pause and notice. When you're working with a part or checking in with yourself, pause and ask: *"What feels different right now?"* Even a tiny change—like feeling 1% calmer—is worth noticing!

What feels different right now?

Example: Not sure. I just feel calmer overall, less reactive to people and situations around me.

____

____

Step 2: Check in with your body. Our bodies often hold onto shifts before our minds even catch up. So, ask yourself:

Is there a place in my body that feels more relaxed or open?

Example: My shoulders don't feel as tense as they used to.

____

____

Step 3: Journal or take notes. Write down anything and everything you notice about yourself.

Examples:
"The anxious part felt less tight today."
"I felt it easier to veer away from what my Firefighter (Mr. Nighttime Snacker) was trying to urge me to do."

____

____

____

____

____

____

Even small shifts are signs of healing. So celebrate even the smallest changes you notice; they're showing you're on the right path.

Dialoguing with Your Parts

After you've unblended from your parts, the next step is usually for **Self to take the lead** and engage with those parts from a place of curiosity, compassion, and calm.

Imagine talking to a child who's afraid of the dark. You wouldn't want to scold them or worse, ridicule them, right? You also wouldn't want to cut them off while they're trying to explain why they're afraid—because in the child's mind the fear is real.

What you'd want is to **soothe** and **reassure** the child first such as holding them close to show them they're safe. Then, once they feel a little calmer, you'd gently set them in front of you so you could see them eye-to-eye.

From there, you'd help them understand that while the dark feels scary, there's nothing there that can really hurt them.

Talking to your parts is just like this.

You don't want to push them away or tell them to stop feeling what they're feeling. Instead, you want to **invite them to sit in front of you**—to make them feel that **Self** is truly there to listen and to understand.

When to Communicate with Your Parts

You can dialogue with your parts in two ways: when they naturally show up in the moment, or in a calm, quiet time.

In-the-moment conversations let you connect with a part while it's active and expressing itself. For example, if you feel a wave of anxiety before giving a presentation, you can pause and ask that anxious part what it needs from you right now.

Calm check-ins are when you engage with a part when things feel settled and you have space to listen without urgency. For example, you might set aside quiet time in the evening to ask if any part wants to come forward and share its perspective about what happened during the day.

So, let's start these dialogues shall we?

Befriending Managers

Managers often carry the voice of pressure, control, and "doing everything right." When you dialogue with a Manager part, you're inviting it to *step out* of its role for a moment and let you see what's really driving it.

How to Dialogue with a Manager Part

- For **in-the-moment conversations**: Let it know you're curious: *"Can you tell me what you're afraid would happen if you stopped managing so much?"*
- During **calm check-ins**: Invite it to share its role in your life: *"I'd like to get to know you better and understand what you're protecting me from."*
- Next, acknowledge its hard work: *"I see you. I know you're working hard to keep everything together, and I want you to know the grown-up me is here to help carry that load."*
- Listen gently to its answers—it might share fears about failure, rejection, or feeling unsafe.

Why this matters: Managers often believe that if they don't stay in control, everything will fall apart. But if you listen without judgment, you're showing them that they don't have to carry this weight alone.

Befriending Firefighters

Firefighters act fast to put out the fires of pain—through distraction, numbing, or intense reactions. They're often misunderstood because their actions can seem impulsive or self-destructive.

How to Dialogue with a Firefighter Part

- **For in-the-moment conversations:** When you notice the urge to distract, numb, or escape, acknowledge it: *"I see you stepping in. Can you tell me what you're trying to protect me from right now?"*
- **During calm check-ins:** Ask about its strategies: *"I'd like to understand how you help me cope when things feel overwhelming."*
- Next, appreciate its intentions: *"I know you're working hard to take my pain away, and the grown-up me is here now so you don't have to do it all alone."*
- Listen with openness—it might share that it's guarding you from intense feelings, memories, or vulnerability.

Why this matters: Firefighters usually act from a place of panic, trying to protect Exiles' raw wounds. When they feel heard and seen, they're more willing to let the Self step in and lead.

Befriending Exiles

Exiles are often the parts of you that feel most alone, scared, or ashamed; they've been carrying deep pain for a long time. Befriending them is about gently letting them know they're not alone anymore.

How to Dialogue with an Exile Part

- **For in-the-moment conversations:** When you feel a wave of sadness, shame, or fear, gently connect. For example, say, *"I sense you're carrying a lot. Can you tell me what it's like for you right now?"*
- **During calm check-ins:** Invite it to come forward if it feels ready: *"I'd like to hear your story whenever you feel safe to share."*
- Next, offer reassurance: *"You're not alone anymore. I'm here with you now—the grown-up me who can protect and care for you."*
- Remember to listen kindly and patiently. Exile parts might reveal deep wounds, unmet needs, or moments of feeling abandoned.

Why this matters: Exiles long to be seen and comforted, but they're often hidden away because the internal family system fears their pain. When you show them patient, compassionate attention, you're helping them feel safe enough to begin healing.

Note: Exiles usually require the deepest and most delicate work in IFS because they carry your most painful wounds and heaviest burdens.

For this reason, the next chapter—Exiles: Meeting Your Hurt Parts with Care—will take a gentler, slower-paced, and more in-depth approach, giving these vulnerable parts the time and attention they need to feel truly safe and understood.

Writing Letters to Parts

Sometimes, it can feel easier to connect with your parts through *writing* rather than trying to engage them in dialogue. Here's why the written word holds unique advantages:

- **Time to Reflect and Organize Thoughts.** Writing gives your Self space to slow down, choose words with care, and explore deeper layers of what a part is feeling—without the pressure or blending that can happen in real-time dialogue.

- **Experiential Benefits.** The act of writing can help Self stay grounded, easing any potential tension and promoting overall well-being. This steady, calm presence makes parts feel safer to share their stories.

- **Empowerment Through Self-Direction.** Writing lets Self set the pace and create a safe container for the conversation, especially when parts are fragile or hesitant to speak directly.

Worksheet 14: Letter Writing to a Part

Step 1: Find a quiet space and take a few slow, steady breaths. (**Tip:** If you have time, engage in Mindful Breathing and Grounding first.)

Step 2: Choose a part you'd like to connect with. It might be a Manager, Firefighter, or Exile that feels especially loud or tender right now. (Just like when trying to talk to a part, your letter can be an "in-the-moment conversation" or a "calm check-in."

Step 3: Start your letter by addressing the part with warmth and respect. You might write:

"Dear Perfectionist Part,"
"Hi, Angry Part,"
"To the little one who feels so sad,"

Step 4: Let your Self speak. You might write:

"I see how hard you're working to protect me."
"I know you're carrying so much pain, and I want to understand it better."
"I'm here for you, and I'm listening."

Step 5: Ask the part what it wants you to know. You could write:

"What are you most worried about?"
"What do you need from me right now?"
"Is there anything you'd like to share that I haven't heard yet?"

Here's some space to write your letter:

____
____
____
____
____
____
____
____
____
____
____
____
____
____
____
____
____

Step 6: Let the part write back. If it feels safe, invite the part to write a letter back to you. First, take a short break—stretch, breathe, or get a drink of water—so you can shift into a more receptive, curious space. When you return, imagine the part holding the pen (or typing) and let it respond in its own words, tone, or even drawings and symbols.

Important: Don't censor, edit, or "translate" what comes out. Let the part's voice be as raw, childlike, guarded, or blunt as it needs to be. The goal isn't to make it sound polished—it's to give the part space to express itself directly. You may be surprised by the clarity, vulnerability, or even humor that emerges.

To give you an idea, here's sample two-way letter exchange showing how Self and a part (in this case, a Manager) might write to each other.

Letter from Self to Part (Manager Example)

Dear Ms. Organizer,

I see how hard you work to keep everything under control. You stay on top of tasks, make lists, and push me to be responsible—often when I'm tired or overwhelmed. I want you to know I'm grateful for the way you've kept things from falling apart.

I'm curious, though—what feels unsafe about slowing down? I'd like to understand what you're protecting me from, so we can find ways to keep me safe without wearing you out.

With care,
Me (the grown-up you can lean on)

Letter from Manager Part to Self

You don't get it. If I stop, everything we've worked so hard for will fall apart.

I'm the one who makes sure you're not judged or seen as lazy. Some people at work are already jealous of you; you know this. So, if you make a mistake and people think you're not good enough, not only will they stop respecting you—they'll be gunning for your job. I can't let that happen. I'm not tired—I can't afford to be tired.

But... if you could promise me no one would think less of us... well, I don't know... maybe I could rest a little.

Here's some space for a part to write back:

Note: If a part isn't ready to write back, that's okay. Some parts may need more time to trust Self before sharing their thoughts directly. In this case, you can simply thank the part for being present, let it know you're here whenever it's ready.

Using Voice Dialogue

Another way to connect with your parts is by using **Voice Dialogue**—a practice where you let your parts speak out loud.

When you speak to and from a part using your actual voice, you can feel their energy and hear their concerns in a more vivid way. This can help you better understand what each part needs and how it's trying to help.

Voice Dialogue can feel a little strange at first, but it's a powerful way to bring more presence and curiosity to your inner world. Think of it this way: we're all already having those inner conversations all the time, right? This is just a practice of having those internal monologues out loud.

Worksheet 15: Voice Dialoguing with a Part

Voice Dialogue doesn't have to be dramatic or long. Just a few gentle exchanges can help you feel more connected to your parts and more able to lead from your calm, compassionate Self.

Step 1: Settle into a quiet space where you feel safe and comfortable. Take a few slow, steady breaths. (**Tip:** If you have time, engage in Mindful Breathing and Grounding first.)

Step 2: Invite a part forward that you'd like to connect with. You might say softly, *"I'd like to hear from the part of me that's feeling anxious/angry/sad, etc.] right now."*

Step 3: Use your voice to speak from the part's perspective. Let your part share how it feels and what it's worried about. You might notice your tone of voice changes—maybe it sounds younger, softer, or more intense.

Step 4: Switch back to your calm, wise Self voice. Let your Self respond with kindness and curiosity. You might say, *"I hear how angry you feel, and I want to understand more."*

Step 5: Go back and forth a few times, letting the part and your Self each have a chance to speak.

When you hear a part's voice out loud, it can feel more real and more separate from your Self. This helps you unblend and see that the part is just one small piece of you, not the whole of you. It also helps the part feel seen and heard—like a child finally getting to speak their truth.

Exiles: Meeting Your Hurt Parts with Care

"The place where you are broken is the place where the light enters." — Adapted from Rumi

A Note Before We Begin: Every part in your internal family system is important. The work of your Protector parts (Managers and Firefighters) are vital; they're often the reason you've been able to keep going, functioning, and surviving all this time.

Their role, however, is more about *prevention* and *deflection*—keeping pain at bay. And for whom? For the Exiles who carry the original wounds that need deeper healing.

This is why this chapter is specifically for Exiles. It will help your Self focus on those very tender parts of you, while still honoring the Protectors who've been guarding them all along.

Exiles hold your deepest wounds—like shame, fear, rejection, abandonment, unexpressed grief or deep sadness. They're the tender parts of you that felt too alone or hurt to share their pain openly.

So while IFS involves understanding Protectors (Managers and Firefighters) and helping the whole system feel balanced, validating and soothing Exiles is often at the heart of the healing journey. So, how does one even begin this sensitive process?

Let's start with a few gentle reminders:

- **There is no "perfect" way to do this.** The only goal is to show your Exiles that they're no longer alone so be gentle, compassionate and patient.
- **You might experience big emotions—or not.** Sometimes, people try this for the first time and experience feelings that catch them off guard. That's okay. If it gets overwhelming, take a break. Still, others are unable to connect with their Exiles and don't feel much—that's completely okay, too! **There's no rush.** Just try again another time.

Now, let's begin...

First, **ensure your Self is in a calm, compassionate and centered place**. If you have a designated Safe Space, go there, but truly any quiet space where you feel safe and comfortable, will do. I suggest engaging in a few minutes of deep breathing at this point.

Second, **gently bring to mind** **The 8 Cs of Self-Energy** (i.e., calmness, curiosity, clarity, compassion, confidence, courage, creativity, and connectedness). Imagine these qualities as a soft light in your heart, a warm presence inside you, or the strong and solid foundations of your Lighthouse.

Next, **invite an Exile part into a conversation** by validating its existence. You might say something like:

"I see you Abandoned One. Your pain is real."
"You know, I'm sorry. I haven't been focusing on you. But I want you to know that I feel you. I hurt with you. I always have."
"You're not alone."

This validation is important because it's like a warm blanket for a part that's been out in the cold for years.

Soothing is the next step. Once the Exile knows you're really there and not going to judge or abandon them, you can offer comfort in gentle, simple ways.

For example, you might close your eyes, place a hand on your heart and say softly, *"I'm here"* or *"I'm ready to listen to you now."*

If you hear or feel nothing back, you might try to **reassure** your Exile part by saying, *"It's okay. I'm here to listen with kindness, not to judge or fix."*

Next, **offer an image of safety**—a cozy room, a gentle light, a lotus flower sitting serenely on a lake–any comforting presence.

This is important, because for many Exiles, being seen and soothed like this is brand new. It's a chance for them to feel how much your calm, wise Self can hold them with compassion.

If no part comes up right away, that's okay. Wait patiently—like waiting for a shy child to feel safe enough to step into the light.

If and when you do sense an Exile part, pause and gently observe. (Tip: Remember your somatic awareness training.)

- *What emotions do you feel as you connect with an Exile part?*
- *Where do you feel it in your body?*
- *How young does my Exile feel?*
- *Does it have a shape, image, or color?*

Important: You don't have to have all the answers—just be open to whatever comes.

After sensing the presence of your Exile, **gently ask**:

"Hello. What are you feeling right now?"
"What do you want me to know about you today?"
"When did you start feeling this way?"
"Is there something you wish someone had said or done for you back then?"
"What do you need from me to feel a little safer?"

Let the Exile part speak in its own way. You might hear words, see images, or feel a wave of emotion. Just keep listening with compassion. (If you want, use Voice Dialogue.)

Once the Exile has shared, offer some kind words of validation. You might say:

"I believe you."
"I sense that this is hard to talk about. It's okay. Just share what feels safe to share right now."
"I see how much pain you're carrying. I'm sorry it's taken me this long to turn to you."
"You don't have to hide anymore—I'm here with you."

Thank the Exile for sharing. Before you end this activity, thank the Exile for trusting you enough to show up. You might say:

"Thank you for sharing this with me."
"Thank you for letting me see this part of you."
"I'm here for you, and I'll keep coming back."

Lastly, **gently return to the present with a few slow breaths**. If you had your eyes closed, slowly open them. Notice the ground beneath you, the weight of your body, and the space around you. Let yourself feel rooted and present.

If meeting and talking to an Exile part has brought up strong emotions, consider:

- Stretching or move your body gently.
- Writing in a journal about what you learned.
- Having a cup of tea or do something comforting.
- Talking to someone you trust.

Important: If you feel triggered or if things feel too intense or confusing, please do not hesitate to reach out to a therapist or trusted professional for support.

Unburdening: Helping Exiles Heal

Imaging seeing a friend you've not been in contact with for a long time. Your first meeting will most likely be casual or "not so deep," right? The same is true when you first meet your Exile parts.

What you've done in the previous chapter is like saying "Hello." No doubt, it's a crucial part in your IFS journey, but it's only the beginning.

This chapter is the next important step—really getting to know your Exiles and helping them reveal to you what's been hurting them for years.

You might start to notice that they're carrying not just unpleasant memories or feelings, but very deep and raw aches and sufferings. These burdens might be something like:

"I'm not good enough, and I never will be."
"I'm broken. I always have been."
"I have to be perfect to be loved."
"I'm ugly. Ugly, ugly, ugly inside-out."
"I'll be rejected if I show how I really feel."
"I'm not worthy to be seen"

Don't be surprised if your Exile's burdens come forth as questions. Sometimes, our deepest hurts come from unmet needs or difficult situations that our younger selves are not capable of understanding. These may sound like:

"Why did they leave me?"
"Why didn't they choose me?"
"What did I do that was so terribly wrong?"

Whatever voice or tone your Exile part uses, remember that the goal of healing isn't to push these burdens out of the picture. It means creating a safe space where your Exile parts can let go of them gently and in their own time.

Worksheet 16: Unburdening

Releasing burdens doesn't usually happen in one single moment. It's often a slow, gentle process. So, let your Exile parts know that there's no rush and that you'll keep coming back to support them, again and again. Each time you do, you're helping them find more lightness, more safety, and more freedom to be just who they are.

Step 1: Start with compassion.

For in-the-moment conversations:
"I can sense you. Do you want to talk?
"I can feel you. Tell me what you're afraid off right now."

For calm check-ins:
"Hello again, is now a good time to talk?"
"Hello Little One, would you like to continue our conversation the other day?"
"Do you feel ready to share your burden?"

Step 2: Reassure.

"You don't need to share everything right now if you don't want to. I'm ready to listen to whatever you want to say."

Step 3: Use imagery. Many people find it helpful to use gentle, healing images when a part is ready to release a burden. The aim is to create a deep sense of safety for your Exile so it feels more willing to let go.

You might want to:

- Picture a tranquil garden where you feel light and your mind is calm.
- Imagine a soft light or a warm, comforting breeze wrapping around you like a gentle embrace.
- Visualize cuddling a pet, feeling its warmth and unconditional love.
- Picture a strong, wise, and gentle hand holding yours, offering reassurance and support.

Step 4: Ask the Exile to write a letter or note to you (optional). Gently ask: *"Would it help if you wrote down your thoughts and feelings?"* If you sense a yes, get pen and paper and let the Exile write down what its burdens feel like or what it believes.

Tip: Some people find it helpful to look at pictures of themselves around the age the Exile first experienced pain or took on its burdens.

When the Exile is done unburdening, consider adding a physical or symbolic action that indicates a release of burdens. For example:

- **Balloon Release**. Take the letter, tie it to a balloon, and then release it into the sky. (Alternative: Release a sky lantern.)
- **Water Ritual**. Take the letter and wrap it around a stone. Walk to a river, lake, or ocean, drop the stone and watch the water carry it away.
- **Fire Ritual**. Safely burn a small piece of paper or image representing the burden, watching the smoke rise and carry it off.
- **Breathing It Out**. Inhale calm, safe energy, then exhale the burden gently, feeling it leave your body with each breath.
- **Blowing Bubbles**. Blow bubbles and imagine the burden being carried away inside them—floating off and popping into nothingness.
- **Burying**. Take the letter or any image representing the burden and bury it in the ground.
- **Shaking It Off**. Stand up after writing the letter, take a deep breath, and then gently shake your arms, legs, or whole body to release any tension or stuck energy the burden holds.
- **Singing or Humming**. Use your voice to hum, chant, or sing softly, letting the vibration carry the burden out of your body.

Why do this? Studies in areas like embodied cognition and somatic experiencing suggests that our bodies and minds are deeply linked. When you act out the release physically, it tells your nervous system: *"I'm really letting this go."*

It helps your brain and body work together to create a real, felt sense of release.[11,12] In other words, it's not just imaginary—your whole system feels the shift. And that's what makes healing feel more real and lasting.

Step 5: Express gratitude and offer comfort and reassurance.

"Thank you for sharing more today. I want you to know that you don't have to carry this alone anymore."
"Thank you for trusting me. Adult me is here. You're safe now."
"I'm so grateful for all you've done to help me. You've been so brave carrying your burdens until grown-up me could arrive. But you can let go a bit now. I'm here."

Important: It truly bears repeating—you might need to do exercise numerous times before full unburdening takes place. Trust is crucial and that takes time to build. Remember, this isn't a race. Go at your own pace.

Navigating Triggers After Unburdening

Unburdening is a milestone in IFS healing and you should be tremendously proud when this happens!

Just pause and absorb this for a moment: your Exile parts have been carrying their burdens (e.g., pain, fear, abandonment, insecurity, worthlessness, shame, etc.) *for years*—and now they're finally beginning to step into a life without that heavy load.

Now, after unburdening, you might notice something surprising: certain situations, people, or sensations can still stir up old feelings. That's okay.

It simply means your system is adjusting to its new balance, and some patterns, especially those wired into your nervous system, need time to update.

Think of it like recovering from a long-standing injury: the pain is gone, but the muscles still remember the limp. But with gentle attention, those patterns fade.

But, why can triggers still show up after unburdening?
Unburdening doesn't mean the complete dissolution or disappearance of burdens. The situation or event that caused the

trauma happened and you cannot go back in time and erase it. So, your Exile parts may still be triggered when faced with these items, people, situations or events. This DOES NOT mean the unburdening didn't work!

When an Exile has been hidden away for years, Protectors have been scanning the environment for anything that might hurt it. After unburdening, Protectors may still react out of habit. And the Exile, even unburdened, might still be startled by reminders of its old pain until it experiences enough safety in the present.

What do you do when your parts are still triggered? Respond as your calm, and wise Self.

Step 1: Stay curious, not alarmed. When a trigger appears, pause and notice it without judgment. Ask internally:

"Which part of me is reacting right now?"
"What does this part need from the grown-up me in this moment?"

This keeps you in Self-energy and reassures your system (1) there's no crisis, and (2) someone is leading or in-charge.

Step 2: Reassure your parts. If the Exile is the one feeling triggered, speak to it gently:

"That was then, this is now. You're safe here with me."

If the Manager is the one feeling triggered, speak to it gently: *"You've worked so hard to keep me safe. But don't worry, grown-up me is here now. You don't have to carry it all alone anymore."*

If the Firefighter is the one feeling triggered, speak to it gently: *"It's okay. There's no need to react. Let's slow down together and find another way"*

Tip: Consider doing Worksheet 16: Unburdening again to reinforce to your parts that its burdens are no longer theirs to carry.

Step 3: Adjust your environment. In the early stages after unburdening, limit unnecessary exposure to strong triggers. For example, avoid revisiting painful places, reduce contact with people who consistently activate old wounds, and be mindful of media (movies, news, or social media) that stirs up intense emotions before your system feels steady.

This isn't avoidance — it's giving your system time to stabilize. As the unburdened part experiences more present-day safety, you can gradually revisit these situations with Self fully present.

Step 4: Practice safe re-exposure. When you're ready, reintroduce mild forms of old triggers in controlled settings. This helps your nervous system rewrite its responses.

For example, if crowds were once overwhelming, start with a small gathering where you feel supported. If certain topics trigger you, explore them gently with a trusted friend or therapist.

Step 5: Create a reassurance plan! Keep grounding tools handy for moments when a trigger catches you off guard. For example:

- Revert to mindfulness exercises (e.g., deep breathing, grounding, nature walking, etc.). Even just a few minutes can return balance and peace into your inner world.
- Carry physical anchors with you (e.g., stone, bracelet, or touch point) that signal *"Adult me is here"* to the triggered part.
- Prepare a short Self-to-part script (written or memorized). For example:

  "I sense your worries. I understand and I'm grateful for everything you've done to keep us safe. But grown-up me is here now, and I want you to know we are safe in this

moment. Now, I will never stop listening you but I'll take the reins now."

Write your Self-to-part script here:

____

____

____

____

____

____

____

____

____

____

Bottom line: Post-unburdening life isn't about erasing what happened in the past or avoiding reminders of them. It's about meeting them with a new, stronger, and more balanced internal team.

So, don't look at triggers as setbacks. On the contrary, they're opportunities to deepen your connection with your parts, strengthen Self-leadership, and build confidence in your system's ability to stay safe, no matter what arises.

Unburdened: A Healing Journey After Release

Every unburdening moment is profound. So, it's not surprising that release often brings a surge of relief, a sense of lightness and freedom that many have never felt before.

In the days, weeks, months, and in some cases, even years that follow, many people find themselves navigating unexpected waves of emotion. Some feel **overwhelmed** by the intensity of what has been let go, or by the sudden quiet that remains where the burden once lived.

Others notice a **sense of emptiness or disorientation**, as if their internal world has been turned upside down.

Protector parts—those who have spent years keeping the burdened part safe—may feel confused or worried. They may wonder what their role is now that the Exile has been freed from its weight. Even parts of you that longed for relief might feel **vulnerable or exposed** in this new, unburdened space.

This chapter is here to help you understand and honor what comes next.

It's an invitation to slow down, to **ground yourself** in safety, and to begin weaving a new relationship with your parts. **Because healing isn't just about releasing what's heavy—it's also about learning how to live with lightness.**

Grounding and Soothing (Yes, Mindfulness again!)

After unburdening, the system often feels raw, open, or flooded with emotions—sometimes even anxious or low in mood. Begin by grounding yourself in the present moment.

Continuously train your Self to live in NOW, not in the regrets of past or the worries of the future. This could be engaging in:

- Deep breathing exercises; not just the ones mentioned in this book but explore other types such as 4-6-8 breathing, alternative nostril breathing, box breathing, etc.
- Somatic movement (e.g., gentle stretching, shaking out tension, or taking regular mindful walks.)
- Connecting with nature or something comforting in your environment.

Integration and Care

After unburdening, Exiles often need time to settle into their new sense of freedom and safety. Support them by creating intentional moments of connection. This could mean speaking gentle, reassuring words, asking how they feel in this moment, and listening without judgment.

You can also offer simple comforts like a warm drink, soft blanket, calming music, or a walk in nature. Most importantly, stay present without rushing them to "be better".

Updating the Protectors

Because the system has operated in a certain way for so long, Managers and Firefighters might feel disoriented.

A common misconception in IFS is that once Exiles are unburdened, Protectors no longer have roles in the internal family. Not true at all. Protectors just need to be assured that their job can *shift* or *soften*.

Meet with each protector individually. Explain, in your own words, what happened during the unburdening and how the Exile feels now. Let them see for themselves that the burden is truly gone.

Reassure them: *"Thank you for all your hard work. Your efforts have been essential to keeping us safe, and we still need you! But now, you can ease a bit and help in a lighter, less tense, and more rewarding way."*

Then, guide Protectors in imagining how their job could shift to:

- **Guiding:** Offering perspective, planning ahead, or helping the system make wise choices without fear driving the process.
- **Encouraging:** Motivating the system to take healthy risks, try new experiences, and celebrate successes.
- **Resting:** Taking breaks, stepping back from constant vigilance, and enjoying the safety they helped create.
- **Advising:** Sharing insights when asked rather than having to control every situation.
- **Collaborating:** Working alongside other parts to maintain balance rather than acting alone.

Bottom line: Protectors will always be parts of your system. They're not being "retired" but "reassigned." Self needs to invite them to shift from survival mode into a more supportive, life-affirming role within the system.

Making Time for Rest

Don't rush. Give your Self and your time to rest and adjust. Let the system settle into its new balance naturally, without pushing or forcing new roles.

Forgiveness: The Gift You Give Yourself

When you work with your Exiles and help them release their burdens, you might find that the idea of forgiveness naturally begins to come up.

Most **Exiles were created from events that were never their fault**—like feeling unloved as a child, experiencing a loss, or living through something that felt too big to handle. Still, "weak," or "unsafe" have become their default vocabulary, and over time, these parts might start to believe they should have been better, stronger, or more lovable. In short, they might carry deep shame or guilt for things that were never in their control.

Forgiveness in IFS is about gently letting these parts know:

"This is not your fault."
"You didn't cause this."
"You're not to blame for what happened."
"You deserve to feel safe and whole again."

Forgiveness is also sometimes about letting go of old anger or resentment toward people who hurt us. This doesn't mean excusing what happened or forgetting it—it means freeing your parts from carrying the heavy weight of those old wounds.

Worksheet 17: The Process of Forgiveness

Forgiveness is not a single moment—it's a gentle, ongoing practice. Here's how you might explore it with your parts:

Step 1: Validate. Before forgiveness can happen, parts need to know you see and believe their pain. So, let them share their story (via a moment of stillness, writing or using voice dialogue) and tell them, *"I believe you. You didn't deserve this pain."*

Step 2: Practice Radical Acceptance. As previously discussed, Radical Acceptance = Reality Acceptance. It's not about "being okay" with what happened. It's about acknowledging that IT happened.

So, you might say to your parts: *"I know this happened; I'm not denying it. We may not like it, and it may still hurt, but we can see the truth of it. And now that we see it clearly, we can begin to heal together."*

Step 3: Acknowledge what was beyond your control. Remind your parts that many of these wounds came from situations that were never their fault. Say softly, *"You were just a child,"* or *"You did the best you could."*

Step 4: Offer self-forgiveness. Many parts feel shame for how they reacted to pain—like hiding, lashing out, or shutting down. Let them know:

- To Exiles: *"You never should've had to carry this, but you did it with such courage. You're free now. There's nothing to forgive—only gratitude and love for you."*
- To Managers: *"You worked so hard to keep me safe in the only way you knew how. Don't blame yourself. You protected us the best you could."*
- To Firefighters: *"You stepped in each time you thought the pain would be unbearable. I understand why you did what you did, and I thank you for caring in your own way."*
- To Self: *"You're forgiven. You were not strong enough then. And you didn't have the tools you have now."*

Step 5: Forgiving others, if and when you're ready. Some parts might feel ready to forgive those who caused them pain. Others might not—and that's okay. Let your parts set the pace. If forgiveness feels safe, you might say:

"I'm letting go of this burden of anger, so I can feel lighter."
"This doesn't mean what happened was okay—it just means I don't want to carry it anymore."
"I extend forgiveness—not because you deserve it, but because I deserve to be free from the burden of what happened."

Integration and Ongoing Practice

"Healing isn't linear. It's a dance between old patterns and new possibilities." — Unknown

As you've been exploring IFS, you've met your parts, learned how to listen and care for them, and practiced leading from your calm, wise Self. Now comes the next step—**integration**.

Integration is about weaving these gentle practices into your daily life, so your Self and your parts can keep growing together in trust, balance, and compassion.

Strengthening Your Internal System

Strengthening your internal system is like caring for a garden. You don't just plant seeds and walk away. You water them, give them sunlight, and watch them grow. In the same way, you can keep checking in with your parts, offering them care, and building trust day by day.

Deepening Your Parts' Relationships

One powerful way to strengthen your system is by helping your parts get to know each other. Parts don't live in isolation; they're members of a family, each with their own worries and hopes.

When you gently help them connect with each other, you create a stronger, more supportive inner world. Here's how to start:

Step 1: Create space for dialogue. Let your parts talk to each other in your mind's eye. Maybe your Manager part wants to tell your Exile it's sorry for being so harsh. Maybe your Firefighter wants to let the Manager know it's tired of always fighting fires.

Step 2: Let Self be the calm mediator. Self is like a kind host at a family dinner, actively listening to each part with warmth and curiosity—not judgment or a desire to "fix" anything. You're there to help them understand each other, not to force them to agree.

Step 3: Notice small shifts. Even a tiny moment of understanding—like a part softening its tone or pausing to listen—can be a big step toward balance.

Step 4: Celebrate connections—big and small! Healing isn't just about reducing conflict. It's also about noticing and honoring moments of cooperation, however small. When you sense your parts listening to one another, sharing space, or stepping back to let another part lead, name it out loud: *"I see how you're learning to work together. I'm proud of you!"*

You might want thank them for specific actions—like a Manager allowing rest time, or a Firefighter pausing before reacting. These celebrations help your parts feel valued, strengthen trust, and encourage more moments of harmony in the future.

Also, do something kind for yourself! Maybe that's making a cup of tea, taking a walk, or listening to music you love. Small celebrations remind your system that healing doesn't have to be all hard work—it can feel good, too.

Building a Harmonious Inner Team

A well-balanced inner team isn't about everyone agreeing all the time. It's about helping your parts feel seen, heard, and understood, so they don't have to work so hard to protect you on their own.

What does a harmonious inner team feel like?

- Your parts don't feel like enemies; they feel like allies.
- You no longer feel like you're being pulled from different angles. You feel calm and steady inside, even when challenges come up.

- Big emotions still arise, but they feel less overwhelming, and there's less urgency to react right away.
- You notice you're less easily triggered, and when something does activate you, you can pause, listen, and respond with clarity instead of reactivity.
- You no longer feel lost. You trust your calm, wise Self to figure things out and lead.

How to Build Harmony

Step 1: Listen to each part's needs. Take time to check in with each part. Ask what it needs and how it wants to help you now. Let each one know you're grateful for its role.

Step 2: Create a safe, open space. Let your parts know that they don't have to fight for your attention. You're here for all of them, and there's room for everyone's voice to be heard.

Step 3: Encourage cooperation. When you sense two parts not getting along, gently invite them to understand each other. For example, suppose a Manager part is more relaxed now, but a Firefighter part still jumps in quickly at the first sign of discomfort.

In this case, ask the Firefighter to share what it's protecting against, and help the Manager listen without judgment. Then ask the Manager to explain its new, calmer approach, so the Firefighter can see there are other ways to stay safe. Affirm that both have the same ultimate goal—protecting the system—and explore how they might share that role in a way that supports harmony rather than conflict.

Step 4: Revisit and reassure. Building harmony isn't a one-time conversation; it's a process. Keep checking in. Remind your parts: *"We're in this together. I'll keep showing up for all of you."*

Building New Habits

As old burdens are released, a profound transformation happens within your internal system. The parts of you that once carried pain or fear finally have space to breathe, explore, and grow.

This newfound openness invites you to build habits and routines that align with who you truly are—habits that support not just your healing, but your wholeness.

This isn't about imposing rigid goals or forcing change. Instead, it's about tapping into nourishing your Self and engaging in activities that truly motivate and inspire you. So, at this stage, I ask you revisit the 8 C's of Self-Energy and the Values Clarification chapters to reconnect with what makes you happy and what you want from life moving forward.

You can also **ask your younger self: "What have you always longed to do?"**

Sit quietly, breathe deeply, and invite your younger self to share their wishes, dreams, and forgotten joys. Maybe it's dancing, painting, singing, exploring the outdoors, or simply resting in stillness. Maybe it's learning something new, reconnecting with old friends, or creating beauty in your home.

Whatever the answers, **listen and honor these inner longings** because these are most likely the ones that can truly light you up inside. For example:

- If your system values **creativity**, you might create a daily practice of drawing, writing, or making music—no pressure, just play.
- If your parts long for **connection**, you might schedule regular check-ins with loved ones or create (or join) a group that shares your passions.
- If your younger self always wanted to **explore**, you might plan small adventures—walking in a new park, visiting a museum, or trying a hobby you've never done before.

Go ahead, and write down your inner longings and how you plant to honor them.

What I long to do:

____

____

____

What I'll do to honor them:

____

____

____

What I long to do:

____

____

____

What I'll do to honor them:

____

____

____

What I long to do:

____

____

____

What I'll do to honor them:

____

____

____

These new habits aren't just tasks on a to-do list—they're expressions of your Self, woven into the rhythms of your life.

Reality Check: No One Supports Me in My IFS Journey

Doing deep inner healing work like IFS can be one of the most courageous and transformative things you'll ever do. But for many people, it can also feel incredibly **lonely**—especially when the people around you don't understand what you're going through, or don't have the same commitment to inner growth.

Maybe you've tried to explain what IFS is—about parts, burdens, and unburdening—and been met with blank stares or even skepticism. Or maybe you've shared how you're feeling after an intense session, only to hear, *"Just get over it"* or *"Why are you so emotional?"* Maybe your friends or family are wrapped up in their own challenges and so come across as uninterested in what you're going through.

Whatever the reason, it's okay to feel frustrated, sad, or even angry about this. **It's natural to long for support and connection in your healing journey.** And it's true: having supportive people around you can make the process easier.

But the deeper truth is that **healing is ultimately an inside job**. It's about you and your parts—no one else can do that work for you. So, here's what to remember if you feel alone:

- **Your Self-energy is your strongest ally.** Even if no one outside of you understands, your Self can still show up with compassion, curiosity, and courage for your parts.

- **You can find support elsewhere.** Maybe it's a new acquaintance interested in mental health, an online IFS community, or an IFS therapist. Even if your immediate circle doesn't "get it," you can always look for support *outside* that circle.

- **This is a test of your commitment to yourself.** Let it remind you that your healing is for you. You're allowed to create a life that honors your inner work, even if others don't see it.

- **Validation doesn't have to come from the outside.** Let your Self and your parts feel your own care and belief in them.

When to Seek Professional Support

While working with your parts on your own can be powerful and healing, there are times when it's wise—and kind—to ask for extra support. A therapist trained in IFS can help you feel safe, stay grounded, and explore your parts more deeply than you might feel able to do alone.

Here are some signs that it might be time to seek help from a professional:

- **You feel overwhelmed or stuck.** If it feels like your parts' voices are too loud, or you're caught in a pattern you can't seem to shift, a therapist can offer gentle guidance and support.

- **Intense emotions feel too much to handle.** If your parts' feelings—like shame, fear, or sadness—are so strong they're disrupting your life or making it hard to function, a therapist can help you feel steadier and safer as you work through them.

- **You're facing too painful memories or trauma.** If your parts' stories involve old wounds, abuse, or traumatic experiences, it's important to have a caring professional to help you navigate those memories safely.

- **You want to go deeper.** Sometimes you're ready for more healing, and a therapist can help you go beyond what you can do on your own—helping you see connections and patterns you might not notice alone.

Asking for help doesn't mean you're failing—it means you're wise enough to know that healing for you may be easier when you don't have to do it all alone.

What to Look for in an IFS Therapist

When you're working with IFS, you want someone who can hold a safe, compassionate space for you and help you connect more deeply with your parts. Here's what to keep in mind as you search for a therapist:

- **Training in IFS.** Look for a therapist who has training and experience in Internal Family Systems. They'll be familiar with the language of parts, Protectors, Exiles, and the Self—and will know how to help you work with them gently and safely.

- **Warmth and compassion.** It's vital to feel safe and cared for with your therapist. Notice how you feel when you talk to them—do they feel warm, kind, and accepting? Do you sense they're genuinely interested in understanding your inner world?

- **Curiosity and non-judgment.** A good IFS therapist will meet your Self and your parts with curiosity and respect, not with judgment or pressure.

- **Comfort with emotions.** Because IFS work often brings up deep feelings, it helps to have a therapist who can hold those feelings with care. They should be able to sit with your pain or fear without trying to rush you through it.

- **Professionalism and clear boundaries.** You want to feel like your therapist can create a safe space for you ethically, while also respecting your boundaries and your pace.

- **Your pace, not theirs.** IFS is not a race, and deep work takes time. Look for a therapist who honors your readiness—someone who doesn't push you to go deeper before you feel safe, and who respects when you need to slow down, pause, or focus on lighter work.

How to Find an IFS Therapist

Finding the right therapist can feel overwhelming at first, but it doesn't have to be. Here's a simple, step-by-step way to start your search:

Search Online Directories. Look for directories that specifically list IFS-trained therapists. Some good places to start:

- IFS Institute Directory: The official list of IFS-trained therapists worldwide.
- Psychology Today: You can search for therapists by specialty and often filter for "Internal Family Systems."
- Local therapy websites. Search for therapist websites in your area; many list IFS as part of their approach.

Ask for Recommendations. If you know friends, family, colleagues, or other health professionals who've worked with an IFS therapist, ask if they have any recommendations.

Interview Potential Therapists. Many therapists offer a free phone consultation. Use this time to ask questions like:

"How do you use IFS in your work?"
"How much do IFS sessions cost?"
"What does a typical session look like with you?"
"How do you help clients feel safe with their parts?"
"I've done IFS self-help at home. How can we build on that work together?"

Notice how you feel talking to them. Do they feel warm, open, and respectful?

Trust Your Gut! You deserve to feel comfortable and seen. If something doesn't feel right, it's okay to keep looking. Finding a therapist you feel safe with is the most important step.

Conclusion

"Healing means accepting all parts of ourselves, not just the parts we like, but all of us." — Louise Hay

Well done you! I hope you'll take a moment to really appreciate yourself. Not in a *"check the box, I'm done reading"* kind of way, but in a deep, quiet way that says, **I showed up for me**. That is what matters.

You've explored the world of Internal Family Systems—meeting your Self, discovering your Protectors, and gently turning toward your Exiles. And you've learned that every part of you has a role, a story, and a reason for being the way it is. None of it is random. None of it is broken.

Now, every single IFS aspect we've covered is important, but there's a rhythm to the work. And I believe this rhythm is:

- **Strengthening self-leadership** so you can navigate your inner world with calm, clarity, and compassion.

- **Gently healing your Exiles**, meeting them with presence, witnessing their pain, and supporting them in releasing the burdens they've carried for too long.

- **Reassuring and reassigning your Protectors** so they can trust that your Self is leading now, and they can take on gentler, more life-giving roles.

Healing isn't a single "aha moment" or a perfectly wrapped ending. It's an **ongoing relationship with yourself**.

Some days will feel spacious and full of Self-energy; others might feel like the old patterns are back in charge. That's okay. Every time you notice what's happening inside you and respond with curiosity instead of judgment or criticism, you are practicing IFS. And every time you practice, you strengthen the trust between your Self and your parts.

So, where you go from here is entirely up to you. You might keep working through the exercises, repeat the ones that feel especially powerful, or simply start noticing your parts more in daily life. There's no wrong pace, no wrong order.

Just remember: your Self is here. Your parts are listening. And every step you take toward understanding and compassion is a step toward lasting change.

Bonus: 35-Day IFS Healing Plan

Welcome to your 35-Day IFS Healing Plan! This plan is designed to help you build a steady and compassionate relationship with your Self and your parts—one day at a time.

This plan is a guide, not a rule book. So, feel free to stay at one stage until ready, repeat weeks, or stretch the plan to 60 days.

Week 1 – Foundation & Self-Connection

Goal: Build awareness of Self-energy and get familiar with your parts.

- **Day 1:** Review the IFS Roadmap, and remind yourself to give yourself patience and kindness.
- **Day 2:** Practice Mindfulness.
- **Day 3:** Practice Radical Acceptance.
- **Day 4:** Practice listening to your body (Somatic Awareness).
- **Day 5:** Read and start to understand your inner family.
- **Day 6:** Draw your IFS Parts Map (before IFS work).
- **Day 7: Rest and reflect.** Practice some light journaling: *"What have I learned about my system this week?"*

Week 2: Deepening Self Work

Goal: Strengthen your relationship with Self so it can guide the healing process.

- **Day 8:** Re-read the 8 C's of Self-Energy. Which quality(ies) do you think you need most work on?
- **Day 10:** Practice unblending. Notice a part and step back into Self-leadership.
- **Day 11:** Take a moment to journal. Ask *"How do I want my Self to lead?"* (Write down the qualities and values that are important to you.)
- **Day 12:** Invite Self to meet one part in a safe inner space.
- **Day 13:** Spend 10 minutes of gentle movement, breathwork, yoga, or anything that helps you nourish Self-energy.
- **Day 14:** Rest and reflect: *"When I lead from my wise, calm, and compassionate Self... what changes inside me?"*

Week 3 – Protector Work

Goal: Build trust with Managers and Firefighters before approaching Exiles.

- **Day 15:** Re-read (or recall) parts of the book that pertain to Protectors (Managers and Firefighters).
- **Day 16:** Dialogue with a Protector: *"What are you protecting me from?"*

- **Day 17:** Negotiate safety. Ask a Protector what it needs from Self to relax.
- **Day 18:** Visualization work. Invite Self and a Protector to observe each other—without judgment or pressure.
- **Day 19:** Journal: *"What my Protectors have done for me."*
- **Day 20:** Encourage cooperation. Introduce two Protectors to each other.
- **Day 21:** Rest and reflect: *"How have my Protectors shifted this week?"*

Week 4 – Exile Work

Goal: Begin meeting Exiles with compassion; no pressure to unburden yet.

- **Day 22:** Read Exiles: Meeting Your Hurt Parts with Care and review safety reminders.
- **Day 23:** Engage in first contact. Describe an Exile you sense (e.g., feelings, sensations, images).
- **Day 24:** Ask an Exile: *"What do you want me to know?"*
- **Day 25:** Witnessing. Try to connect with an Exile and stay present while the Exile shares its story.
- **Day 26:** Try to connect with an Exile and offer comfort, e.g., a safe place imagery, soothing words, or supportive presence.
- **Day 27:** Journal: *"How my relationship with an Exile part is changing."*

- **Day 28:** Rest and reflect. Practice self-soothing activities (e.g., self-hugging, deep breathing, nature walking, etc.) if emotions feel stirred.

Week 5 – Unburdening & Integration

Goal: Support release (if ready) and build harmony across your system.

- **Day 29:** Guide an Exile through an unburdening visualization or repeat comfort practices if an Exile part is not ready. (**Note:** You may need to try this step numerous times over days, weeks or months—and that's okay!)
- **Day 30:** Re-read Navigating Triggers after Unburdening and create your safety re-assurance plan.
- **Day 31:** Update Protectors about changes in your internal family system. Re-assure them and guide them into their new ways of thinking and helping the inner family.
- **Day 32:** Check-in with your Self, visit each part, and see what's needed—forgiveness, reassurance, gratitude, or simply your Self's calm presence.
- **Day 33:** Journal: *"How is my internal family system doing this week?"*
- **Day 34:** Engage in an activity that celebrates your inner family—as it is right now.
- **Day 35:** Draw a new IFS Parts Map (after IFS work).

A Little Help?

Hello! If you've found this workbook helpful, healing, or even just comforting to read, I'd love to ask for a *small favor* that makes a *big difference*.

Even just a few sentences about your favorite exercise, an insight you gained, or how it made IFS feel more approachable can help others decide if this is the right resource for them — and it helps me keep creating tools like this.

How to help: Please visit this link: https://amazon.com/review/create-review?&asin=B0G1TGV7VX or scan the QR code on this page.

***Note**: If you're from outside the US, please update the link above from amazon.com to your country code (e.g., amazon.co.uk, amazon.ca, amazon.de, etc.). Using Kindle or an e-reader? Scroll to the bottom of the book and swipe up to prompt the Review page.*

THANK YOU FOR YOUR HELP!

Ava Walters

SCAN ME

About the Author

Ava Walters is the founder of LifeZen Publications. Coming from a family with a history of mental health issues, her journey began as a personal quest to find balance, inner peace, and what we all desire—happiness. This pursuit has led her to explore traditional psychotherapeutic methods and diverse holistic practices.

She has an MBA with a specialization in International Project Management (IPM). However, her trajectory took a significant turn after experiencing "burnout and a breakdown." She then returned to her first love—writing, complementing it with her deep passion for psychology. This transformation marked the beginning of her new journey. One focused on unraveling the intricate connections between human behavior and mental healing.

When she's not writing, Ava can be found on her yoga mat, taking long nature walks with her husband, or in the kitchen, constantly experimenting with new recipes to her husband's delight.

Learn more about Ava and LifeZen Publications here:
https://life-zen.com/

Recommended Reading

The RADICAL ACCEPTANCE WORKBOOK

Best For: Anyone who struggles with self-criticism, guilt, emotional pain, or current life circumstances. This workbook is ideal if you're ready to release resistance, practice deep self-compassion, and create peace with what is—even when life feels unfair or out of your control.

Click here to get this book: https://amzn.to/3XXuiGI

Click here to get the audiobook: https://amzn.to/4g2SzDm

The ACT THERAPY WORKBOOK FOR ADULTS

Best For: Adults looking to better handle difficult thoughts, emotions, and life stressors using Acceptance and Commitment Therapy (ACT). Perfect if you want to live more in alignment with your values while managing overwhelm, avoidance, or emotional paralysis.

Click here to get this book: https://amzn.to/3WMsnUC

Click here to get the audiobook: https://amzn.to/3XGrPRL

The ACT THERAPY WORKBOOK FOR ANXIETY RELIEF

Best For: Anyone dealing with daily stress, anxiety, panic attacks, or chronic worry. This workbook is designed to help you step back from anxious thoughts, build emotional resilience, and take grounded action—even when feeling overwhelmed.

Click here to get this book: https://amzn.to/4c1FCID

Click here to get the audiobook: https://amzn.to/4hJkisD

The ACT, DBT & CBT WORKBOOK FOR OCD

Best For: Anyone struggling with obsessive thoughts, compulsive behaviors, or overwhelming rituals. This workbook offers a blend of ACT, DBT, and CBT approaches to help you break free from the cycle of OCD, find calm, and build a more flexible, fulfilling life.

Click here to get this book: https://amzn.to/4iB9SvC

Click here to get the audiobook: https://amzn.to/3RYTfPj

SOMATIC THERAPY WORKBOOK (Just 10 Minutes a Day)

Best For: Anyone feeling stress, tension, overwhelm or "out of sorts" in their body and want body-based techniques to address them. This workbook offers 70+ easy somatic exercises that can offer relief by calming your nervous system, releasing stored tension, and helping you feel more grounded and present.

Click here to get this book: https://amzn.to/412Xwq0

Click here to get the audiobook: https://amzn.to/4m8kqok

DBT SKILLS WORKBOOK FOR TEENS (Gamified!)

Best For: Tweens and teens struggling with "adulting" in today's world. Adopting a gamified approach (there are quests!), this workbook is full of relatable stories and activities to help them learn important life skills—all while keeping the process fun, engaging, and rewarding.

Click here to get this book: https://amzn.to/4lDUv7P

References

1 Ruggiero, G. M., Spada, M. M., Caselli, G., & Sassaroli, S. (2018). A historical and theoretical review of Cognitive Behavioral Therapies: From structural self-knowledge to functional processes. *Journal of Rational-Emotive & Cognitive-Behavior Therapy*, *36*(4), 378–403. https://doi.org/10.1007/s10942-018-0292-8

2 Madsen, P. (2024, August 17). *Is Internal Family Systems (IFS) evidence-based? Understanding its role*. Sea Change Psychotherapy - Atlanta Counseling. https://seachangepsychotherapy.com/posts/is-internal-family-systems-ifs-evidence-based/

3 Haddock, S. A., Weiler, L. M., Trump, L. J., & Henry, K. L. (2016). The efficacy of Internal Family Systems therapy in the treatment of depression among female college students: A pilot study. *Journal of Marital and Family Therapy*, *43*(1), 131–144. https://doi.org/10.1111/jmft.12184

4 Hodgdon, H. B., Anderson, F. G., Southwell, E., Hrubec, W., & Schwartz, R. (2021). Internal Family Systems (IFS) therapy for posttraumatic stress disorder (PTSD) among survivors of multiple childhood trauma: A pilot effectiveness study. *Journal of Aggression, Maltreatment & Trauma*, *31*(1), 22–43. https://doi.org/10.1080/10926771.2021.2013375

5 Frühauf, S., Figlioli, P., Oehler, D., & Caspar, F. (2015). What to expect in the intake interview? impression management tactics of psychotherapy patients. *Journal of Social and Clinical Psychology*, *34*(1), 28–49. https://doi.org/10.1521/jscp.2015.34.1.28

6 Nickerson, C. (2024, January 29). *Impression management: Erving Goffman theory*. Simply Psychology. https://www.simplypsychology.org/impression-management.html

7 Ackerley, R., Hassan, E., Curran, A., Wessberg, J., Olausson, H., & McGlone, F. (2012). An fmri study on cortical responses during active self-touch and passive touch from others. *Frontiers in Behavioral Neuroscience, 6.* https://doi.org/10.3389/fnbeh.2012.00051

8 Edwards, D. J., Young, H., Curtis, A., & Johnston, R. (2018). The immediate effect of therapeutic touch and deep touch pressure on range of motion, interoceptive accuracy and heart rate variability: A randomized controlled trial with moderation analysis. *Frontiers in Integrative Neuroscience, 12.* https://doi.org/10.3389/fnint.2018.00041

9 Hawkley, L. C., & Cacioppo, J. T. (2010). Loneliness matters: A theoretical and empirical review of consequences and mechanisms. *Annals of Behavioral Medicine, 40*(2), 218–227. https://doi.org/10.1007/s12160-010-9210-8

10 Hoffmann, A. (2020). Humans are not meant to live alone. *European Journal of Preventive Cardiology, 28*(16). https://doi.org/10.1177/2047487320920757

11 Wu, L., Huang, R., Wang, Z., Selvaraj, J. N., Wei, L., Yang, W., & Chen, J. (2020). Embodied emotion regulation: The influence of implicit emotional compatibility on creative thinking. *Frontiers in Psychology, 11.* https://doi.org/10.3389/fpsyg.2020.01822

12 Payne, P., Levine, P. A., & Crane-Godreau, M. A. (2015). Somatic experiencing: Using interoception and proprioception as core elements of trauma therapy. *Frontiers in Psychology, 6.* https://doi.org/10.3389/fpsyg.2015.00093

www.ingramcontent.com/pod-product-compliance
Lightning Source LLC
Chambersburg PA
CBHW050524240926
51846CB00003B/691
* 9 7 8 9 0 8 3 5 7 5 4 2 1 *